MW00852802

ÆFTER STOICISM

ÆFTER STOICISM

Last Words of the Last Roman Philosopher

THOMAS M. WARD

Published by Word on Fire Academic, an imprint of Word on Fire,
Elk Grove Village, IL 60007
© 2024 by Word on Fire Catholic Ministries
Printed in the United States of America
All rights reserved

Cover design and interior art direction by Nicolas Fredrickson,
typesetting by Clark Kenyon.

Unless otherwise noted, Scripture excerpts are from the Revised Standard
Version of the Bible, copyright 1952 [2nd edition, 1971] by the Division of
Christian Education of the National Council of the Churches of Christ in the
United States of America. Used by permission. All rights reserved.

No part of this book may be used or reproduced in any manner whatsoever
without written permission, except in the case of brief quotations in critical
articles or reviews. For more information, contact Word on Fire Catholic
Ministries, PO Box 97330, Washington, DC 20090-7330 or email
contact@wordonfire.org.

First printing, October 2024

ISBN: 978-1-68578-133-0

Library of Congress Control Number: 2024937322

To Torrey

Contents

Preface

This book tells the story of a man whose long study of philosophy had given him respectable answers to all of life's hard questions. Then life happened. He was a high-ranking Roman senator and cultured man of letters, wealthy and well-connected, happily married and a father to children he admired. He was as privileged as they come. Then he was accused of treason, convicted without fair trial by the Gothic king who had been his friend, and sentenced to death. Awaiting his execution in prison, he withered in despair.

The man's name is Anicius Manlius Severinus Boethius (480–524 AD)—or simply Boethius, as he is usually called. He is the greatest Roman philosopher of the sixth century AD. That might not sound like a great accomplishment if your mental timeline includes the sixth century in the so-called "Dark Ages." But he really was an excellent philosopher, and in his day probably knew more of the history of philosophy than anyone else in Western Europe. As, not for the last time, the lamps were going out all over Europe, the Last Roman Philosopher did his part to make sure that history was not lost.

Somehow, though deep in depression, Boethius found it within himself to survey the whole course of his life (even the darkest parts), come to see it as good, and die in hope. But this was no psychological miracle. His mind was full of the wisdom of the past, stocked over decades of study. In the barren time, he looked within and found a feast of words to give him hope. We need to do our part, for ourselves and for future generations, to make sure his story is not lost, and to make his hope our own.

The wisdom that Boethius has to share is in large part the wisdom of the ancient philosophical movement known as Stoicism: through the practice of the virtues, we can achieve a tranquility of mind that is imperturbable despite the ups and downs of fortune. It holds out the hope of a life free of suffering. But Boethius has more to offer. He goes beyond Stoicism by affirming all that is wise in that venerable tradition but aiming higher, showing how true happiness and not just the absence of suffering can be the object of reasonable hope.

LAST WORDS

A book called *The Consolation of Philosophy* comprises the last words of Boethius. He wrote this book in prison, awaiting execution. Though little read today outside of the ivory tower, it exerted enormous influence on centuries of Western thought and culture. A literary and philosophical masterpiece in its own right, it is also at least equally important as a conduit, from antiquity through the Middle Ages, of a whole way of looking at the world—a worldview—different in so many ways from our own. As a scholar, I have one foot in ours and another in his. My hope for this book, then, is to make that worldview intelligible and attractive, and to invite readers to struggle toward the hope it has fostered in so many people in the millennium and a half since *Consolation* was written.

A NOTE ON *CONSOLATION*

The Consolation of Philosophy is *prosimetric*—that is, composed of alternating prose and meter (poetry). *Consolation* is divided into five books, and each book is divided into several sections.

Typically, for each prose section there is a poetry section—only the end of book 1 and the end of book 5 break this rule. When I'm referencing a prose section, I add a "p" next to the section number (e.g., 1.1p), and if a poetry section then an "m" (e.g., 1.1m).

My own book contains many references to *Consolation*. Reference without quotation is indicated by "C" for *Consolation*, followed by the section number (e.g., C 1.1m). For quotations, I have mostly used the translation by Scott Goins and Barbara H. Wyman. Page numbers following a section number refer to their translation (e.g., C 1.1, 2). Quotation from a different translator is indicated by the translator's last name followed by page numbers of his or her translation (e.g., C 1.1, Watts, 3).

1

The Whole Garment

STRANGER THINGS

I went to a public high school in Southern California, and after graduating with pretty good grades, I still had never so much as heard of Boethius, let alone read *Consolation*. The only book from the so-called "Dark Ages" that we were ever assigned was *Beowulf*, which is not bad and bears some traces of influence by *Consolation*. But my classmates and I were assigned another book about a man in prison awaiting his execution. It was by a Frenchman, Albert Camus, and it was published in the amazingly enlightened twentieth century, in the middle of World War II.

This book, called *The Stranger*, tells the story of a man named Meursault, whose mom has just died and whose amoral apathy gets him involved in an acquaintance's squalid domestic dispute. His involvement ends when he shoots a man on the beach in broad daylight. His first shot is lethal. But then he shoots four more bullets into the man's body, just because. After his conviction for murder, he is sentenced to death. To the priest who comes to visit him, he exclaims that the fact that each of us is going to die means that our lives are meaningless. A man's life matters no more than a dog's. There is no responsibility, there is no judgment. Nothing matters. Meursault says all this in a rage, hands at the priest's neck. Prison guards rescue the priest, who departs in sorrow, leaving the prisoner alone.

Some find the ending of *The Stranger* grimly comforting, a sort of mysticism for naturalists. "I laid my heart open to the benign indifference of the universe," and finding it so much like himself (that is, benignly indifferent), he feels that he is happy and has led a happy life. He concludes the novel with a declaration of his one ultimate hope, that "on the day of my execution there should be a huge crowd of spectators and that they should greet me with howls of execration."[1] We will see by the end of this book the grounds of Boethius's hope for rather more than howls of execration.

If we consider the history of philosophy from the middle of the twentieth century to the present day, Camus (1913–1960) and his sometime-friend Jean-Paul Sartre (1905–1980) have good claim to be among the philosophers most influential on the broader culture. When they are celebrated, it is for their efforts to imagine the conditions for living a subjectively fulfilling life in a world that is objectively meaningless. They believed the most important of these conditions was authenticity, and authenticity was, in their eyes, the condition that civilization itself had been built up to suppress. Anything that the subjective individual could ever feel as external imposition on how to conduct one's life is, for that very reason, an enemy of authenticity and must be opposed. Everything from basic manners and etiquette to moral obligations and religious authority has to go.

While we enjoyed generational connections to the world they hated, their influence was limited and they could be appreciated as a sort of corrective voice of contradiction, like an old court jester. But they did their work too well. The grandparents of the millennials are dying out. We are all existentialists now, and we can hardly bear it. Most of us would rather not forge our own existence but grow into the full measure of who and what we are under the tutelage of the inherited wisdom of countless generations

1. Camus, *The Stranger*, trans. Gilbert, 154.

of humans trying to human well, mediated to us through these civilizing institutions.

But we don't realize just how much has been taken from us. So our longing for the stability of cultural inheritance is currently manifesting as a mania for remakes: from *Cinderella* to *Ninja Turtles*, it seems that every story you or your parents knew as kids is making a comeback. The hugely popular Marvel and DC films draw on the ancient repository of comic book characters going all the way back to the 1930s but whose heyday was the 1960s. In early 2023, Warner Bros. announced its plan to make new *Lord of the Rings* films—and Peter Jackson's famous films, themselves adaptations of Tolkien's great story from the 1950s, are barely twenty years old. Our taste for nostalgia may not be new, but the newness of what we can collectively feel nostalgic about is peculiar.

But not everyone has forgotten the deep past. As we grope ahead into our post-postmodern future, many are looking back centuries, not decades, for guidance. The scholarly project of re-membering the great sages of the past is, thankfully, beginning to find major expression outside the ivory tower. There is a wide-spread yearning to reconnect with our past and invite it to inform how we live our lives today. "Ask for the old paths, where is the good way, and walk therein, and ye shall find rest for your souls."[2]

TAKING RESPONSIBILITY

King Alfred the Great (849–899) is among the great figures of history who changed his world for the better by looking to the old paths. The welfare of the Anglo-Saxons needed more than just hard-won peace with the Vikings. Knowing the importance of education and religion for civic flourishing, Alfred undertook a revival of both. He recruited eminent scholars to come to his

2. Jeremiah 6:16 (King James Version).

court and establish a culture of learning in his lands.[3] Alfred himself learned to read and write, and even learned Latin. His translation of *Consolation* is the first in (Old) English, and the first in a vernacular language. Probably Alfred had some assistance in preparing his translation. But it's less important to know his precise degree of Latin prowess than to know that as this good king was trying to refound civilization on the isle of Britain, *Consolation* was one of about half a dozen books he and his advisors prioritized in their translation project.[4]

Doubtless part of the appeal of *Consolation* to the king of the Anglo-Saxons lay in its promise that while there are many things we cannot control, we do have control over our own actions and our own characters. If a good life is measured not primarily by one's fortunes (which we cannot control) but by one's character (which we can), then, difficult as life may be in ninth-century Wessex or twenty-first-century America, we can still forge good lives: noble, purposeful, fulfilling. This is one of the most important themes of *Consolation*, and it is the part of *Consolation* that has the most affinity with Stoicism.

In our own time, as many of us are following in the footsteps of Alfred by looking to the past as a source of wisdom for living well, Stoicism has become, by far, the most popular ancient school of thought. The contemporary public philosopher Ryan Holiday's Stoic trilogy—*The Obstacle Is the Way*, *Ego Is the Enemy*, and *Stillness Is the Key*—has sold several million copies. Mark Manson's pair of crassly titled books, which we can shorten to *The Subtle Art* and *Everything*, have sold even more copies. Manson's central concept, "not giving a [dang]," is basically a modern translation of the Stoic concept of *apatheia*, which is a kind of cultivated detachment that helps us remain unperturbed through life's roller coaster. And there are dozens of similar books and websites,

---

3. Sedgefield, *King Alfred's Version of the Consolations of Boethius*, xiv.
4. Phillips, "The English Tradition of Boethius's *De consolatione philosophiae*," 222–24.

higher-brow, lower-brow, for kids, for parents, for intellectuals, for bros, all explaining and recommending a Stoic way of life.

But I suspect that Stoicism appeals to us for reasons different from Alfred's and the Anglo-Saxons'. We live in comparative luxury and peace. It is easy to become complacent and self-indulgent in times like ours. It is easy to become soft and to find discomfort intolerable. It is also easy to become spoiled, blaming whatever we think are our problems on everything but ourselves.

Obviously, moral obligation and our many dependencies on each other make us partially responsible for each other. There is a lot of wisdom, for example, in being able to take a look at anyone convicted of a crime, even a capital crime, and see not only the individual criminal but the community that let that person down, see that in some sense we together have produced the criminal. But I suggest that this is no longer an urgent lesson for society to learn. It is now a well-entrenched component of our collective wisdom.

Again, obviously our bodies, including our brains, sometimes pose significant obstacles toward maintaining that sense of life as good and meaningful. Deeper understanding of the physiological basis of forms of mental suffering like depression and anxiety has been helpful for many people, myself included. But here too, it is no longer urgent for us to be told over and over that "mental illness is like any other medical illness."[5] It may even be harmful.[6] It is perhaps more important to hear that we are not our brains, and that except in extreme and rare cases, having a mental illness does not obliterate our ability to make choices and take action.[7]

The lesson we need to relearn is how much really is in our control—what *truly belongs to us*, in the idiom of the Stoics— and what we are therefore personally responsible for. And that is

5. Malla et al., "Mental Illness Is Like Any Other Medical Illness."
6. Saxbe, "This Is Not the Way to Help Depressed Teenagers."
7. Schwartz and Gladding, *You Are Not Your Brain*, 21.

where the Stoics are so helpful. If human happiness depends on anything *outside* us, then we are bound to be miserable. This is because everything outside us is something we either *will* lose or something we *can* lose. (In this sense, even good health, including good mental health, is something "outside" us.) So even if we get exceptionally lucky and ride a wave of good fortune our whole lives, still our happiness will be marred by the knowledge that we *might* lose our good fortune, and that we *will* die, and by the fear following on that knowledge. So real happiness, if it is possible, must not depend on these losable goods of fortune.

I think most of us understand this, even if we find it challenging to live it out. A more difficult lesson for people like us is how to deal with misfortune. If good fortune is not what makes us truly happy, shouldn't it follow that bad fortune is not what makes us truly unhappy? Yet we struggle to draw the inference. Our unhappiness, we think, is not the sort of thing we have control over. Instead, our unhappiness is due to other people or classes of people. Or it is due to our mental or physical health problems. Or our lack of resources. Or, or, or.

But notice the fallacy here. We already agree that good fortune doesn't guarantee happiness. But if you didn't have any of the misfortunes listed above, you'd have very good fortune indeed—and that wouldn't be enough to make you happy! It follows that whatever is really responsible for your unhappiness is not your bad fortune but something else.

The Stoics identified one of the secret ingredients of the happy (or unhappy) life. It's you.

THE STOIC MOMENT

Stoicism began at the end of the fourth century BC, when its founder, Zeno of Citium (334–262 BC), started teaching his philosophy in the Stoa Poikile, a grand sort of covered patio in the Agora, or town center, of ancient Athens. Zeno's teaching career began not long after the close of a triple-generation of philosophical greatness extending from Aristotle (384–322 BC) to his teacher Plato (428–347 BC) to his teacher Socrates (469–399 BC). So towering were this trio that, a couple hundred years later, the shrewd Cicero (106–43 BC) could with some justification complain that everything truly insightful about Stoicism could already be found in Aristotle and Plato[8]—an antique equivalent of A.N. Whitehead's (1861–1947) famous twentieth-century quip that the whole history of Western philosophy is "footnotes to Plato."[9]

The charge has some justice when it comes to ethics—our main focus here—but really shortchanges the Stoics, especially their most brilliant exponent, Chrysippus (279–206 BC), with respect to the two other fields of inquiry the Stoics really cared about: logic (or dialectic) and physics (or natural philosophy). Recent scholarship makes a powerful case that Gottlob Frege's (1848–1925) groundbreaking work in logic in the nineteenth century was, after all, dependent on Stoic antecedents[10]—and Frege is widely regarded as having brought an end to two thousand years of Aristotelian hegemony in logic.

In physics, the Stoic doctrines of strict physical determinism and pantheism owe more to Heraclitus (540–480 BC) than Plato or Aristotle.[11] And long before Friedrich Nietzsche (1844–1900) popularized eternal recurrence as a therapeutic device, the Stoics boldly proclaimed a literal eternal recurrence: never-ending time punctuated by conflagrations in which everything burns, the world is reconstituted, and history repeats itself, over and over again.[12]

8. Cicero, *De finibus* 5.1.
9. Whitehead, *Process and Reality*, 39.
10. Bobzien, "Frege Plagiarized the Stoics."
11. Long, *From Epicurus to Epictetus*, 266.
12. Sandbach, *The Stoics*, 78–79.

But it is for their contributions to ethical theory and practice that the Stoics enjoy such high esteem today. They have little to say about social or political thought, but they have a great deal to say about how to conduct our lives individually. In short, theirs is an ethic of personal responsibility. That their ethical vision does not ramify out to political philosophy is most definitely a limitation, but it is not necessarily a fault. There is much to learn from the Stoics if we focus on what they focused on rather than what they did not.

Stoic ethics, as with all ethical thought from classical antiquity, starts with the question, *how do I live a truly flourishing life?*[13] Its focus then is primarily on well-being or happiness, not duty or law.

Stoics teach that without personal virtue—good moral character—no one can be truly happy. Without *temperance*, your natural desires for food and drink and sex will overwhelm your life. Without *justice*, you will defraud other people and live in fear that they will try to do unto you as you do unto them. Without *prudence*, you will not be able to think well either about how to achieve your goals or even what to aim for. And without *fortitude*, you will not be able to persevere through those inevitable difficult times. Thus, even if you happen to enjoy excellent health and wealth and all the external goods for which most folk pine, without virtue you will be incapable of enjoying these in a way that is actually good for you. Moreover, without virtue, you will live in a state of fear and anxiety, lest your goods be taken from you. Finally, without virtue, if and when these goods are taken from you—and you can be sure they will be—you will be miserable for the loss of them. Virtue therefore gives you the capacity to enjoy external goods without being too attached to them; Stoics call this state *apatheia* or the correct emotional detachment from the kinds of goods that you can lose.

13. Annas, *Morality of Happiness*, 27.

Stoic detachment helps you recognize that the good things you enjoy are not after all the foundation of your happiness. Stoic happiness is not what we would think of as ecstasy or bliss or euphoria, but more like tranquility or serenity (*ataraxia*)—even keel, come what may. And when, either at death or sometime before, you are forced to part with your external goods, you are not miserable for the loss of them but acknowledge they were never yours to begin with and were never truly under your control. So the Stoics teach not just that you need the virtues to be happy—they add that with the virtues, you have all you need for happiness. This is the foundation of the radical Stoic claim—faintly echoed by Immanuel Kant (1724–1804) many centuries later—that only virtue is unconditionally good.[14]

In their insistence that the virtuous person can be happy in any circumstance, Stoics don't mean that you can trick yourself into finding unpleasant things pleasant, as though roadkill could start smelling like roses if you tried hard enough. Instead, they recognize that while many things in life are hard, how we react *to*, and act *in*, difficult circumstances is in large measure *up to us*. You can let your bad fortune overcrow your spirit and leave you sad. Or you can not let it. "I am condemned to death. Do I have to die moaning and groaning as well? To incarceration. Do I have to complain about it?"[15]

Unfortunately, the vast majority of the writings of the early Stoics, including Zeno and Chrysippus, have been lost. For what remains of their work, we are dependent on fragments and reports scattered throughout the works of later philosophers and historians such as Cicero, Diogenes Laertius (180–240), and Johannes Stobaeus (fifth century AD). But there are also eminent later Stoics, some of whose complete works we do still possess. Among these are several who are nearly household names:

14. Cicero, *De finibus* 3.3.

15. Epictetus, *Discourses* 1.1.22, in *The Complete Works*, trans. Waterfield, 72–73.

9

Seneca (4 BC–65 AD), Epictetus (55–135), and Marcus Aurelius (121–180)—the latter surely the most famous not only because of his great book, *Meditations*, but also because he was emperor of Rome and, well (you know I have to say it), was the father of the evil emperor Joaquin Phoenix—I mean Commodus—in Ridley Scott's hugely popular film *Gladiator*.

Boethius's *Consolation* is saturated with references and allusions to Stoic authors.[16] Usually, these authors are not explicitly quoted but instead woven seamlessly into the fabric of the *Consolation* itself, as though they were as familiar to Boethius as pop music and internet memes are to so many of us. *Consolation* is a book that couldn't have been written without Stoicism, but it is not a Stoic book. Boethius is a philosopher who belongs to no particular school. He learned from all of them. In fact, he seems to have read everything there was to read. But he was no dilettante. He was a real philosopher with the humility to read widely from the wise men of the past but also the boldness and creativity to do original work.

LADY PHILOSOPHY

Boethius was also one of those rare people who seem to be able to do more than one thing really well. Born into a cultured and prominent senatorial family, Boethius would himself grow up to be a politician, but a politician who led a scholarly life—or was it a scholar who led a political life? Actually, it's hard to say. We know from his books he was a talented scholar; it seems from the historical records that he was a talented politician. Boethius's father and grandfather served terms as consuls, and Boethius himself and his two sons after him followed the family tradition. After his father's death, Boethius, still a boy, was taken into the household of Symmachus (d. 526), *paterfamilias* of an even more

16. Gruber, *Kommentar zu Boethius*, 458–520.

cultured and prominent senatorial family, into which he eventually married. His term as consul came in 510, and in 522 he was appointed Master of Offices, an administrative post one historian describes as a hybrid between head of central intelligence and personal secretary to the emperor—or, in Boethius's own day, to the Gothic King Theoderic (454–526).[17]

Amid all the toil of politics, Boethius kept up his intellectual interests. His philosophical life was not a mere hobby. In fact, he saw his intellectual work as part of his political work, part of the way he would serve the common good. In his commentary on Aristotle's *Categories*, he said, "Although the cares of my consular office prevent me from devoting my entire attention to these studies, yet it seems to me a sort of public service to instruct my fellow-citizens in the products of reasoned investigation."[18]

So close to power, so committed to philosophy. We have in Boethius something approaching the ideal of the philosopher-king of Plato's *Republic*[19]—as Boethius himself recognized (C 1.4p). The problem, however, is that Boethius was neither king nor emperor, and shared his power with fellow senators, hardly any of whom had the philosophic disposition. Boethius would eventually be forced to choose between the moral idealism of philosophical life and the cynical pragmatism of political life. We know the choice he made. Of his efforts transmitting Greek philosophy to his Roman peers, Boethius said, "I shall not deserve ill of my country in this attempt."[20] His country begged to differ.

It was his role as Master of Offices that really forced Boethius into the rough and tumble of Roman politics. King Theoderic was not a pagan but an Arian, that is, a follower of the heresy of Arius, according to which Jesus Christ is not God—a heresy

17. Chadwick, *Boethius*, 46.
18. Boethius, *In categorias Aristotelis* 2, in Troncarelli, "New Words on Boethius," 7.
19. Plato, *Republic* 5 473c–d. All Plato references found in *Complete Works*, ed. Cooper.
20. Boethius, *In categorias Aristotelis* 2, in Troncarelli, "New Words on Boethius," 7.

that proved hard to kill despite its condemnation long before at the Council of Nicaea in 325. From Constantinople, the Eastern Emperor Justin I (450–527) contemplated strategies for bringing what remained of the Western Empire under Byzantine control. When they looked east, Boethius and his fellow senators could see both the idea of Rome and the orthodox faith still in ascendancy. It would have been impossible not to be sympathetic.

Theoderic had pursued a policy of religious toleration, letting the non-Arians and their pope practice their own religion. But that policy had to be reexamined under Justin's reign. The new emperor worked hard for the unity of orthodox Christians in the East and West, brokering a resolution of a temporary schism between Eastern and Western orthodox Christians in 519. Constantinople once again looked to Rome for religious leadership. It was intolerable that the pope should be at a heretic's mercy for the exercise of his ministry. Would Justin attempt to liberate the Italian peninsula? Theoderic became suspicious. He lost trust in some of the senators, or at least the ones who were more than nominally religious. Like Boethius.

And also like one of Boethius's fellow senators, Albinus. This pious man may or may not have been conspiring with some of Justin's officers against the king. But a lower secretary named Cyprian wanted the king to believe that he was. Albinus was denounced. The king convicted him without trial, then accused the whole senate of complicity in Albinus's alleged treason.

Boethius had to do something. And he had to do the right thing. Rising from his seat, he addressed the king: "Cyprian's accusation is false. But if Albinus did it, both I and all the senate have acted with a single counsel. It is false, my lord king."[21]

Could Boethius have guessed what this short speech would cost him? Maybe. But then again, he might have liked his chances. He and Theoderic knew each other well. Boethius knew

21. *Anonymus Valesianus* 2, in *Boethius*, trans. Chadwick, 48.

Theoderic couldn't govern without the senate. And Boethius himself was a big deal—Master of Offices—and knew it. It was without a doubt a brave thing to do, but there is some reason to think that Boethius did not believe as he chose his words that his defense of Albinus would cost him his life. Brave, but not (yet) heroic. In fact, at one point Boethius comes close to expressing regret for getting involved at all: "Surely you recall how I defended them all with no regard for my own security. . . . But you see what results my innocence has brought. Instead of receiving the rewards of true virtue I suffer the penalty of a crime I didn't commit" (C 1.4p, 21).

The rewards of true virtue. Boethius understood a lot about true virtue, but he deeply misunderstood its rewards. Until that fateful day at court when he rose to refute Cyprian's accusation, life had gone exceedingly well for him. The practice of virtue and the enjoyment of all of fortune's favors went hand in hand. What a pleasant life! Until it wasn't. And Boethius's world was undone. He was quickly tried and sentenced to death. He endured a stint in prison, in Pavia, long enough to compose *Consolation*. Historical records do not tell us what sort of prison he was confined in. It may have been a dungeon or it may have been more like "house arrest." But we know he wasn't enjoying the comforts of his own home, because *Consolation* testifies that he no longer had access to his home library (C 1.5p). Wherever he was, he knew that with every page he wrote, he drew closer to violent death.

He was still in his early forties when he died. But already he finds himself "in old age's gloom. Old age came unsought:/ hastened by evil, commanded by pain. / With hair whitened, and skin trembling loose, / my worn frame shakes" (C 1.1m, 4). Beauty faded, body sore, he longs for death. But not like one of his heroes, Socrates. Socrates looked forward to his death as the gateway to closer communion with the gods.[22] True philosophy,

22. Plato, *Phaedo* 63e.

he said, is to practice for dying and death. But all Boethius wants right now is to be free from pain. His inner monologue is one long complaint. He even complains that death "refuses to close my weeping eyes." Now that Fortune has "changed her cheating face," his "wicked days drag forward endlessly"; indeed, his whole life has to be reinterpreted in light of his downfall: he has never been happy (C 1.1m, 4–5). Call no man happy until he is dead, Solon taught.[23] One swallow does not make a spring, nor does a short time make us happy, added Aristotle.[24] Boethius is entirely bereft of hope.

And then his guest appears to him in prison, unexpectedly and suddenly, quite close, towering over his head. It was a woman, her face youthful but also full of years. Her eyes a piercing fire. Boethius, the greatest living philosopher in all of Europe, did not recognize her. She was Lady Philosophy.

REPAIRING THE GARMENT

There are three paradoxes about Lady Philosophy that we learn almost as soon as we meet her. There is the paradox of age: "Her face was vital and glowing, yet she seemed too full of years to belong to this generation" (C 1.1p, 6). Every reader of Tolkien will here remember the Elves. Of Arwen Evenstar it was said that "her white arms and clear face were flawless and smooth . . . yet thought and knowledge were in her glance, as of one who has known many things that the years bring."[25] But Boethius the author would have been thinking rather of gods, and specifically Athena of the flashing eyes, goddess of wisdom.[26] Possibly also of Sophia (i.e., Wisdom) in the Bible, who says of herself that "the

23. Herodotus, *The Histories* 1.30–3.

24. Aristotle, *Nicomachean Ethics* 1.7 1098a. All Aristotle references found in *The Complete Works of Aristotle*, 2 vols., ed. Barnes.

25. Tolkien, *Lord of the Rings* 2.1, 227.

26. Homer, *Iliad* 1.194–222 and *Odyssey* 6.14–81, 14.187–440, as noted in Boethius, *Consolation*, trans. Goins and Wyman, 5n6.

Lord created me at the beginning of his work, the first of his acts of old. Ages ago I was set up, at the first, before the beginning of the earth."[27] And yet just a few lines down she's establishing a home like a young farmer's wife: Wisdom has "built her house . . . slaughtered her beasts, she has mixed her wine, she has also set her table."[28] And maybe he was thinking even of the mysterious woman in *The Shepherd of Hermas*, who appears to Hermas sometimes as an old woman and sometimes as young.[29]

There is the paradox of height: "Her height was hard to tell; at one moment it was that of any ordinary human, but at another she seemed to strike the clouds with the crown of her head" (C 1.1p, 6). We all know the cliché about having one's head in the clouds. That might go all the way back to Aristophanes, who ridiculed philosophers and especially Socrates for his devotion to celestial things: in one play the character Socrates says of "the clouds of heaven" that they are "goddesses of men of leisure and philosophers. To them we owe our repertoire of verbal talents: our eloquence, intellect, fustian, casuistry, force, wit, prodigious vocabulary, circumlocutory skill."[30] A little more seriously, there is also the priestess Diotima, who instructed Socrates that the true way of love—contrary to the imaginations of his drinking buddies—led up through our earthly loves into heaven.[31] The author might also have had an even more solemn image in mind: the extremely tall woman in the Bible, often associated with the Blessed Virgin Mary, the "great portent" who "appeared in heaven, clothed with the sun, with the moon under her feet, and on her head a crown of twelve stars."[32] One of Mary's devotional titles is "Seat of Wisdom."

27. Proverbs 8:22–23.
28. Proverbs 9:1–2.
29. *The Shepherd of Hermas* 18, in *Apostolic Fathers*, ed. Holmes, 209.
30. Aristophanes, *The Clouds*, in *Four Plays*, trans. Arrowsmith, 46.
31. Plato, *Symposium* 201d.
32. Revelation 12:1.

And most importantly, there is the paradox of her dress. Lady Philosophy wove it herself. It was made "of the finest thread, skillfully woven and imperishable" (C 1.1p, 6). It's not the sort of garment that moth and rust can corrupt. But for all its imperishability, it has been damaged: "This same garment had been ripped by the hands of some violent men, who had torn away from it what bits and pieces they could" (C 1.1p, 6). If violent men can rip away pieces of her dress, it seems to follow that the dress is not imperishable. Rip enough pieces away and there is no more dress.

But the paradox of height might help to resolve the paradox of the dress. Lady Philosophy's height knows no bounds. Remember how Aslan looked bigger to the Pevensie children when they returned to Narnia? "'Aslan,' said Lucy, 'you're bigger.' 'That is because you are older, little one.'"[33] Boethius is old in the ways of philosophy, but in his current state he has forgotten who he was. To his grief-drunk sight, the Lady appears to shrink and grow, haphazardly. If he had clear sight, wouldn't she grow taller the more he grew in wisdom? If so, then her gown really is imperishable, however many pieces violent men rip away.

Wisdom is endless. One man's portion of wisdom is not. To paraphrase Heraclitus, the eternal Logos that makes us wise is infinite and available to all, but most people live as though their wisdom is their own.[34] T.S. Eliot made this philosophical fragment an epigraph to his poem *Four Quartets*, in which he tells us that "The only wisdom we can hope to acquire / Is the wisdom of humility: humility is endless."[35] The problem with the violent men is their pride. They thought they'd found the whole of wisdom. But they had only a tatter. They claimed the tatter as their own, ignorant of the endlessness and so imperishability of Lady Philosophy's dress.

33. Lewis, *Prince Caspian*, in *The Chronicles of Narnia*, 380.
34. Heraclitus 10.2, in McKirahan, *Philosophy Before Socrates*, 116.
35. Eliot, "East Coker" 2, *Four Quartets*, 27.

But who are these violent men? Lady Philosophy doesn't name names, but she does name schools. Socrates and Plato are named as model philosophers, and Socrates especially—not in spite of but because of his martyrdom for Philosophy's sake. But after Socrates, "the Epicurean and Stoic herds and all the rest tried to snatch his legacy, every man for himself. They grabbed me, too, as their prey while I shouted and struggled against them, and they ripped this garment of mine, which I had woven myself. As they went away with some little shreds torn from it, they thought that I had yielded myself completely to them" (C 1.3p, 12). These are difficult words to read. It's best not to treat them blithely. Those who tear at Lady Philosophy's dress have violated her, defiled her.

Wait, Stoicism? If you don't know much about Epicureanism, don't worry, we'll get to that later, in chapter 3. But Stoicism? Isn't that the view that says we shouldn't worry about what fortune brings us, good or bad, because true peace of mind is not dependent on fortune but on our own virtuous character? What could be bad about that? How could such a philosophy be likened to a violation of Philosophy herself?

The first thing to say is Lady Philosophy evidently considers at least some Stoics her followers. Only a few lines after accusing the "Stoic herds" of violence against her, she singles out two Stoics for special praise. So her condemnation of Stoicism can hardly be a blanket condemnation of everyone everywhere who has claimed Stoicism for their own philosophy. Instead, the problem she is getting at is school-mentality, identifying oneself so much with a school of thought that one cannot receive wisdom from any other school. This mentality is what nowadays we would call ideology. Philosophy's greatest enemies, those violent men, are those who in the name of Philosophy confine themselves to an ideology and teach others to do the same.

For all Stoicism's merits, it didn't get everything right. It tilts fatalistic—no room for free will. It envisions our highest happiness as the mere absence of suffering. And it encourages a ghastly sort of detachment even from close friends and family. Boethius was attuned to these problems and offers us resources for embracing the best of Stoicism while avoiding its pitfalls. Under the guidance of Lady Philosophy, he learns to say to the Stoics that "there are more things in heaven and earth . . . than are dreamt of in your philosophy."[36]

Lady Philosophy knows that Boethius is bound to suffer. She has come in part so that this innocent man should not have to walk his path alone (C 1.3p). No torn tatter will suffice. Boethius needs the whole garment of Philosophy, not this or that philosopher. Boethius, the man and the author, portraying himself in his book as the prisoner he really was, summons a thousand years of philosophical thinking to help him remember who and what he is and what he can hope. When Boethius the character first sees the Lady, he doesn't recognize her. She wipes his tears with her dress. Finally he sees. "When I cast my eyes upon her and fixed my gaze, I saw it was the one whose home I had visited since my youth—the Lady Philosophy, my nurse" (C 1.3p, 11). His cure had begun. And ours can too.

36. Shakespeare, *Hamlet* 1.5.66–67, p. 96.

2

Philosophy as Therapy

DOCTOR AND PATIENT

Lady Philosophy is a rare thing: a doctor of philosophy who can help people. It's easy to make fun of doctors of philosophy. And it's good for doctors of philosophy to make fun of themselves. There are actually some funny moments in that ambitious flop of a film *Treasure Planet*. In one of them, Captain Amelia, Dr. Delbert (PhD), and Jim are hiding from the mutinous crew of the RLS *Legacy* and their savvy chief, John Silver. Amelia has been injured in a blast. Jim, still just a kid, turns to the grown-up in the room and demands Delbert do something for her. Exasperated by his own impotence, in sharp contrast to *Star Trek*'s Dr. McCoy, he shouts back, "Dang it, Jim. I'm an astronomer, not a doctor. I mean, I am a doctor, but I'm not that kind of doctor. I have a doctorate. It's not the same thing. You can't help people with a doctorate. You just sit there, and you're useless."

I've been in professional philosophy for a while now, and my sense is that many of us in the guild think philosophy is pretty useless. But that's not necessarily a bad thing. "Useless" is said in several ways. In one way, the useless is whatever is worth doing for its own sake. This sort of thing isn't useful for anything; it's just the top-of-the-line type of activity in the doing of which human potential is fully realized. Think about certain experiences of listening to music, or seeing great art, or being in nature; think

19

about special moments with your closest friends and family; think about times when you have been moved to give thanks, or to praise or adore. At our best, these are useless activities. A lot of academic philosophy might be like this.

But in another way, the useless is what doesn't matter, or what is unimportant, trivial. In fact, this sense of useless is almost the complete opposite of the other kind. The other sense of useless is what's worth doing for its own sake; this sense is what's not worth doing at all. A lot of academic philosophy is definitely like this.

Before his downfall, Boethius had spent long hours in his personal library, luxuriously appointed in glass and ivory (C 1.5p). There, he puzzled over the most technical aspects of philosophy and mathematics and music theory, composing groundbreaking and highly influential commentaries on Aristotle and Porphyry and Aristarchus. In the formation of European civilization, *Consolation* was unparalleled: "In its Latin original and its several translations into virtually every European language, it represented a best seller in the Western world for more than a thousand years."[1] But his more technical work in logic, metaphysics, and music was at least as influential in those subjects as *Consolation* was in the broader culture. It is said that Boethius's *De Institutione Musica* remained "the most authoritative work on musical theory for almost a thousand years.[2] Surely, these arcane pursuits belong in one or the other category of useless.

I think they do. Happily, the former. But it is good to remember Boethius was at least as much a public servant as he was a private scholar. He saw his scholarly work, even the technical stuff, as ordered to the common good of the Romans. Whether that ambition was naive is beside the point. I see no reason to suppose that Boethius was insecure about the worthiness of his work. I'm sure he knew it was worth doing for its own sake. At

1. Reiss, *Boethius*, ii.
2. Reiss, *Boethius*, 24.

the very least, we all have at least a little leisure, and a man needs a hobby. But it's a good thing to know about him, and a point in his favor, that even at the peak of his good fortune, he already had a conception of philosophy as the kind of thing that can help people.

Lady Philosophy had no need of a doctoral degree. But she is a doctor, and the kind that can help people. Boethius, the author, working out his issues, decides to write a book. It's going to be a book of philosophy that offers his own most reflective answers to life's hardest questions before he dies. A philosopher with deep roots in the great books, he decides to make it literary, dialogical, and dramatic, with a bit of narrative structure. He himself will be a character. He won't be the one helping others—friends, Romans, countrymen—instead, he will be the one who is helped. In fact, he'll abase himself in print, no self-flattery, no holding back. He will show in writing his need for a hero. And somehow All of Philosophy (the whole garment) will be his dialogue partner. Drawing on antecedents of personified wisdom, the image of a Lady begins to take shape.

What will she be like? What sort of personality? The artist asks questions like these and starts to fill in the details: young and old, tall and short, dressed with an imperishable but tattered and sooty dress. To this triplet of paradoxes, the author adds one more, which is hardly paradoxical at all to anyone who has had a mother: she will be ferocious and tender, just as ready to rebuke and insult (therapeutically) as she is to comfort.

Why make Philosophy out to be like this? Ignoring the literary antecedents, what is it about All of Philosophy that made it seem fitting to Boethius to condense and depict it as a regal matronly nurse?

The obvious answer is that Philosophy can help people: by giving them what they need if not always what they want. The therapeutic benefit of Philosophy need not be its only justification. Maybe it really is worth doing for its own sake, by completely virtuous people with a lot of time on their hands. And for a big chunk of his life, Boethius was that guy. But then he wasn't. And the thing in him that always reminded him that his scholarly studies weren't merely for his own edification but for the good of Rome, now shouted that Philosophy was not just something one could do as a flowering of high culture but something one could receive as medicine for the soul.

"The therapist assumes that the client experiences anxiety that stems from some existential conflict, often unconscious, related to guilt, choice, commitment, self-awareness, freedom, isolation, loss, meaninglessness, and death. . . . Imminent death, or the thought of time running out, propels individuals into a personal confrontation with their existential situation in the world."[3]

It is likely that Boethius's political life was not a daily grind until 522 when he became Master of Offices. He would not have had as much time for study. It is possible that the wise voices who spoke to him through his books grew quiet as he found himself more and more in court and less and less in the library. This would explain why virtuous Boethius so utterly lost it after his conviction, sentencing, and imprisonment. Whatever his prior reading might have prepped him for, at the moment of crisis he was not in a position to remember well.

In his existential crisis, he found himself turning to anything but Philosophy. And this is why Lady Philosophy has to clear the room before she can triage.

MUSING OURSELVES TO DEATH

"Who let these whorish stage girls come to see a sick man? It's more pain they bring than remedies. No, they are making things worse with their sweet-tasting poison. These are the kind of

3. McDougall, "What Role Philosophy in Psychotherapy," 3.

women that choke off a mind's rich fruit, wrapping it up in sterile thorns of passion. They make a mind more used to disease, instead of setting it free from pain" (C 1.1p, 7).

These are Lady Philosophy's first words. The "whorish stage girls" (*scenicas meretriculas*) are the Muses of Poetry (*poeticas Musas*). They had been giving Boethius "words to suit his tearful mood," when Philosophy barges in. She says their words are a poison that cannot truly comfort or cure, only drug him to complacency about his sickness.

We know in advance, by the book's title, that Lady Philosophy is going to be the heroine, but we shouldn't be too quick to root for her. And this seems like a bad first impression. I can think of lots of times when a movie or novel or music brought some comfort; you can too. An old favorite is a song by Laurie Hyde-Smith called "Me and Willie," made famous by Emmylou Harris. The song tells the story of a pair of country singers who tour around from bar to bar playing their music. It's narrated from the perspective of Willie's female partner and focuses on Willie's gifts as a singer-songwriter, as well as his tragic weakness for booze.

Willie's songs really hit people. Of one, she says that it would "tear your heart right out." Willie could "take a crowd of rowdy drunks and hush 'em with a song." He "had a way of lettin' go, making blue turn gold." Moist poignantly, he could "take the blues right out of you, and put 'em in a song."

Aristotle wrote about the power of tragedies to bring catharsis, that feeling of released tension as we move from identifying with the hero's aspirations, virtues, and flaws, witnessing the havoc wreaked by those flaws on the hero himself and those around him, then leaving the theater with our emotions and judgments more closely aligned with the moral order and the order of nature.[4] Tragedy, therefore, can be cleansing or purifying.

4. Aristotle, *Poetics* 6 1449b.

So can a good song. You got those blues in you; you put on a sad song, and your blues go into the song.

But this isn't as simple as it sounds. When you're hungry, you might reach for a candy bar instead of a banana. The candy bar (let's say) tastes better than the banana, and it satisfies your hunger. Later on, you get hungry again, and again go for the candy bar. And over and over again you keep choosing the candy bar. Each time (let's grant), it satisfies your hunger. But that's not all it's doing. It's making you want it again and again, even when you're not hungry. Your candy diet is destroying you. You become blotchy, obese, achy, diabetic. The momentary benefit of each candy snack is far outweighed by the gigantic harm you are doing to yourself.

It's like this with songs and many other artworks, especially our culture's other favorite medium, film. Each artwork (let's grant) is fine to enjoy, and in the moment does for you what you want it to: have a good cry, vicariously trounce your enemies, laugh, glimpse a little hope. For treating some pain or restlessness or anxiety, these can help. But they play as powerfully on our emotions as sugar does on our tastebuds: you keep wanting more than is good for you because it feels good.

Willie's songs didn't do much good for him, by the way—or his partner. She "never understood how he played so good / while drinking himself half-blind." They "watched a lot of dreams die young." Eventually, she decides to leave him "in a bar in Marietta / Couldn't stand to watch the man I love drink himself to death." But Willie and his tear-your-heart-out songs were all she had. She had no mental resources to build a different and better life. She moves to Ottawa and gets a normal job. But "the good life don't look so good from behind a desk."

In *Amusing Ourselves to Death*, Neil Postman explained his mentor Marshall McLuhan's key insight in this way: "The clearest way to see through a culture is to attend to its tools for conversation."[5] Postman laments (in 1985) that television had fundamentally changed the way in which discourse is conducted. TV turns everything into commercial entertainment, not just our storytelling but all our discourse. And what's not amenable to television goes by the wayside. So, we lose touch with cultural artifacts that are often difficult to learn to enjoy but are better for us, and fail to sustain the cultural conditions for producing future masterpieces. We are sick as a result. The internet has made things worse.[6]

It is not the enjoyment of the poetry the Muses inspire that is so bad for Boethius; it's the steady emotional feeding on their words, like spending hours a day in front of a TV or on your phone, or like an exclusive diet of candy bars or beer. Lady Philosophy is not calling for an end to poetry. She herself sings many songs in her efforts to cure Boethius, and her first song is an elegy at least as pathetic as the song Boethius was singing when she stole into his cell. Banishing the muses, then, is not some sadistic effort to make poor Boethius's final days as insipid or as miserable as possible. Instead, it's temporarily needed to reawaken that part of Boethius's soul by which alone he can find true happiness in his suffering, and to align that poetic impulse with ruling reason.

In this way, Lady Philosophy is doing for Boethius what "her Plato" had Socrates do for his friends in *Republic*: Socrates banishes the artists from his ideal city, only to craft an artwork himself, the elaborate Myth of Er.[7] As he makes clear, the problem is not with poetry as such but with poetry that makes "pleasure and pain . . . kings in your city"[8]—where the city is *Republic*'s big metaphor for the soul. "The pitying part [of the soul], if it is nourished and strengthened on the sufferings of others, won't be

---

5. Postman, *Amusing Ourselves to Death*, 8.
6. Carr, *The Shallows*.
7. Plato, *Republic* 10 608c–621d.
8. Plato, *Republic* 10 607a.

easily held in check when we ourselves suffer."[9] Boethius's over-indulgence has him weighed down, "neck pressed with chains"—like the prisoners in Plato's allegory[10]—"face cast down, / forced to discern nothing / but the ground" (C 1.2m, 9). The best art leads us up out of our suffering. It directs our gaze upward to noble and true things, not downward to the world of shadows and smartphones. It keeps us light and fit enough to fly. So, before she begins to diagnose the sickness of which his self-indulgent poesying was just a symptom, Lady Philosophy's first task is to cancel his Netflix and Spotify subscriptions.[11]

THE FIRST DIAGNOSIS

The Muses gone, Lady Philosophy can get to work. "When half-gods go," Emerson said, "the gods arrive."[12] Now one on one, she takes a fold of her dress and dabs Boethius's weepy eyes (C 1.2p). This helps him see well enough to recognize who she is.

It is hard to sustain a philosophical life, or even an intellectual life. Hardly anyone has very many hours of leisure to pursue serious reading, thinking, writing, and conversation with friends about ideas. Unless you are a professor or a fellow at a think tank or are independently wealthy, you shouldn't be too hard on yourself about how difficult it is to carve out time to think. But that doesn't mean you have no responsibility. You might not need saving from the hysterics, as Boethius did, but you might need saving from distraction. Can you recognize philosophy?

We must think of Boethius as a man with a decent education, but now so far removed from his studies that he cannot immediately recover a philosophical way of thinking. The touch of Lady Philosophy's dress is almost like the way that simply being around

---

9. Plato, *Republic* 10 606b.
10. Plato, *Republic* 7 514a–517a.
11. McCracken, "Should You Quit Netflix?"
12. Emerson, "Give All to Love," in *Poems*, 9:84–85.

books tends to inspire all but the dullest people. Even if you're not much of a reader, walk into a good bookstore or library, smell the paper, see each facing spine like the veil of a world, the bookcases galaxies, and you will find that part of you that longs for wisdom like a young Solomon.

The touch of the dress was enough to steady Boethius. But her dress is not as powerful as the robe of Jesus, touching the mere hem of which cured the woman diseased with an issue of blood.[13] Boethius was now able to recognize Lady Philosophy for who she is, but he was still far both from her and from himself.

In *Till We Have Faces*, C.S. Lewis's (1898–1963) retelling of the myth of Cupid and Psyche, Psyche's sister Orual's world is undone first by the loss of her sister to the god Psyche—in whose existence she claims not to believe—and then by her sister's exile to a life of solitary penitential wandering after Psyche's disobedience of the god's one fairy-tale command—a disobedience imperiously encouraged by Orual herself. After the loss of her sister, Orual lives out a whole life of stern impersonality, face veiled, brutally efficient queenship, all to keep herself from probing the wounds of her sister's torment and her own role in bringing that torment about.

Apparently accidental circumstances of her life prompt her to begin to explore her past, in writing. It takes shape as a long complaint against the gods, for their indifference, their cruelty, their bad sense of humor. She is given the grace to give a speech to the gods in which she will be free to make her complaint. She begins to read her story. She expects it to be as she has written it: eloquent, thorough, just. But at the tribunal, she receives the terrifying revelation that instead of her vindicatory story, her autobiography is just "a vile scribble" scratched by a savage hand.[14]

---

13. See Matthew 9:20–22.
14. Lewis, *Till We Have Faces*, 331.

Orual had a story to tell about herself. And it wasn't the right story. That is the shocking and humiliating thing about autobiography: it is way, way harder than we think it is. Sure, you might be able to tell a good story. Whether it really is the story of your life is another matter. Self-knowledge doesn't come cheap.

Lady Philosophy asks Boethius what's wrong, and he gives a very long speech about how dedicated he has been to Philosophy and Roman politics. Like the great philosophers before him, he has attended to his studies and has tried to do good in the world. He has been rewarded only by treachery and suffering. He closes his speech with a beautiful song, one of the most important of the whole *Consolation*. The God in whom he still believes governs all the seasons and all the ways of nature, but man is a surd: "All things obey their ancient law / And all perform their proper tasks; / All things thou holdest in strict bounds,— / To human acts alone denied / Thy fit control as Lord of all" (C 1.5m, Watts, 15–16).

It is natural to respond to injustice with an urge to make things right. The will to power that manners can make dormant revs to life: Something must be done! You must do something! This urge is a desire for things to conform to your will, and the sense of permission to act on that desire is rooted in the conviction that it is not you yourself that demands the conformity, but justice itself, with which your will for once is aligned. You would thwart the evildoer's acts of free will, good as free will is, for justice's sake.

Have you ever wanted your own freedom to be taken away, to free you to do always and only what is right? Have you ever felt not only others' freedom but your own as a burden to yourself and others and the world? Wouldn't it be better if that whole freedom thing could be taken away? (I have felt this.)

That is what Boethius wants, in his song. He wants human affairs to conform to the orderly motion of the planets—on earth as it is in heaven. In expressing this desire, Boethius shows that he is still suicidal. For what he is longing for is for human beings, himself included, not to be human. To foreshadow: we know that Boethius is healing when much later on, after Lady Philosophy has discoursed eloquently about the providential order of things, he asks how there can be room for freedom in such an order! (C 5.2p). But for now, he feels the gift of freedom only as a burden, or curse.

Lady Philosophy listens placidly. His speech and perhaps especially his song helps her to see his sickness: he has forgotten who he is. Wicked men have stripped him of his status and his possessions, and in his illness, he judges that all is lost. In his poem, he had said plaintively that all things (but man) obey their ancient law. Now Lady Philosophy gently rebukes him, echoing a metaphor from Marcus Aurelius:[15] he is a citizen of an imperishable city, whose "oldest law" is that "any man who has chosen to make his dwelling there has the sacred right never to be banished" (C 1.5p, Watts, 17).

Zena Hitz adapts the ancient image for our own time: in a chaotic and often hostile world, a rich intellectual life creates a sort of fortress or refuge against fortune's vicissitudes, where the inside can be bigger than the outside. It is "hidden" not in the sense that it is wholly private (there is a whole city inside) but in the sense that it does not reside out in the open for all to see.[16] Here you are free. If you make this fortress your true home, you can never be banished; and since the cities and lands from which you can be banished—e.g., Rome or Los Angeles—are not your true homeland, your banishment need not break your heart or spirit.

If a man really and truly thinks he is a kitty cat or a piece of glass, we rightly judge him to be mentally unwell. He has

15. Marcus Aurelius, *Meditations* 2.16.
16. Hitz, *Lost in Thought*, 54–87.

identified with something with which he is not identical. But this is precisely Boethius's problem! And it is our problem too. We identify with things that we are not: jobs, possessions, status, even our feelings. You are not any of these things, any more than the sick man is a piece of glass. That is the gist of Lady's Philosophy's first diagnosis: Boethius has incorrectly identified himself; he has forgotten who he is: a philosopher dedicated to a life of virtue.

This is bad enough, but according to Lady Philosophy, it is not Boethius's only or even his worst illness.

THE WORST DIAGNOSIS

Identification is perilous, now more than ever. Contemporary culture offers two sources of authority about what we really are, two sources of authority that do not sit well together. On the one hand, it is supposed to be up to the individual to identify for himself (or herself or themself or . . .) what he (or she or they or . . .) really is. On the other hand, it is supposed that science alone can disclose what we really are. Where the individual alone is in charge of identity, we leave room for those historically unusual self-identifications of the sort now familiar to us all due to the success of the transgender movement. Where science reigns, we risk reducing the human animal to something merely animal, or merely chemical, or merely physical—as longevity entrepreneur Bryan Johnson puts it, "I'm a collection of 35 trillion cells."[17]

These sources of authority license different and competing conceptions of our relationship to our bodies. The scientistic source implies that the relationship between our selves and our bodies is strict identity: there is nothing more to us than whatever non-reducible physical structure there is to our bodies. But where the individual is recognized as an authority over identity, there is an implicit but strict non-identity between our selves and our

17. Johnson, quoted in Klee, "Millionaire Biohacker."

bodies: what we really are is in no way determined by our bodies, and since we happen to have bodies, it ought to be up to us either to make our bodies whatever we want them to be or (where this is not feasible) to try to live (and demand others cooperate with our efforts to live) as though our peculiar bodily conditions are irrelevant to our identities.

Boethius and Lady Philosophy implicitly urge us to reject both sources of authority over our identities, along with both sorts of relationships to our bodies these sources imply.

A few years ago, it was national news that Rachel Dolezal, the former president of a regional chapter of the National Association for the Advancement of Colored People, was a white woman. She identified as black. Many refused to endorse her self-identification. The ground for this refusal was not the color of her skin. Instead, it was the fact that, as a white woman, no matter how she styled her hair or what organizations she joined, she could not have the experience of being viewed as and treated as a black woman. She could not really know what it is like to be black.

As many noted at the time, there is an interesting parallel between a white woman's attempt to identify as a black woman and a man's attempt to identify as a woman. If we refuse Dolezal's racial self-identification on the ground that her skin color kept her from sharing the full black experience, shouldn't we also refuse a man's self-identification as a woman on the similar ground that his sex keeps him from sharing the full experience of being a woman?

The conversation highlighted how confused we are about identity. We all agree that there is something peculiar about human beings that opens up a wide range of permissible lifestyles. Our own preferences and dispositions and perhaps above all our own free will really do seem to have an important part to play in determining what sort of life we will live. The Sorting Hat takes our preferences into account, Harry Potter explains to his son Albus, who is scared he will be placed in Slytherin House.[18]

But our freedom to self-identify is not absolute. This is obvious, even trivial. The hard part is to have some principled way of drawing boundaries. If you think a man is a woman if he thinks he is but that a man is not a goldfish even if he thinks he is, what puts woman within, and goldfish without, the boundaries of what a man can be? One sort of answer is that only those categories that are "socially constructed" are or should be within the range of options individuals can choose. Thus, since having been alive for fifty years or being five feet tall are not the sort of facts that are socially constructed, they are not within my range of options. But maybe being a man or being a woman is socially constructed. "One is not born, but rather becomes, woman," according to the modern proverb.[19] Then I am free to choose, or should be free to choose.

If there is anything plausible to the hypothesis that socially constructed categories are the categories with which it is possible for an individual to identify simply by wishing to do so, then a new conceptual challenge is to find a principled way to distinguish socially constructed categories from those that are not. And this is quite difficult to do, as the Dolezal case makes plain.

The second widely accepted source of authority is science. Using the term "science" in this way is admittedly blunt. For one thing, science claims no such authority for itself; instead, those do so who subscribe to an ideology known as scientism. For another thing, science is not monolithic. If we look at humans only through the lens of biochemistry, they will look rather different than they would if we looked only through the lens of physics. Science as such, then, offers no single theory about what we are. What scientistic accounts of our identity have in common,

---

18. Rowling, *Harry Potter and the Deathly Hallows*, 758.
19. De Beauvoir, *The Second Sex*, trans. Borde and Malovany-Chevallier, 330.

however, is the tendency to reduce the human person to what can be known through empirical methods. Those who grant science the last word suppose that what science cannot illuminate is illusory.

The most extreme sort of reduction is to suppose that we're just particles. "Fermions and bosons. All the processes in the universe, from atomic to bodily to mental, are purely physical processes involving fermions and bosons interacting with one another."[20] Since fermions and bosons cannot explain morality, or free will, or meaning, or God, those who believe that these particles are all that exists are forced to admit there are no such things as morality, freedom, meaning, or God.

A less extreme sort of reduction tells us we're just our body parts. In *Pilgrim's Regress*, C.S. Lewis tells the story of a young man named John, who is imprisoned by a wicked giant called Spirit of the Age. The giant's enchantment over the prison makes the prisoners appear to one another as though they had no skin: "A woman was seated near him, but he did not know it was a woman, because, through the face, he saw the skull and through that the brains and the passages of the nose, and the larynx, and the saliva moving in the glands and the blood in the veins: and lower down the lungs panting like sponges, and the liver, and the intestines like a coil of snakes."[21]

John is rescued from this prison by a lady in shining armor whose name is Reason. But even after his rescue, John is shaken by his horrible vision of what, he supposes, we really are: ugly lumps of organic material. Lady Reason corrects his mistake: Spirit of the Age "showed you by a trick what our inwards *would* look like if they were visible. That is, he showed you something that is not, but something that would be real if the world were made all other than it is."[22]

20. Rosenberg, *Atheist's Guide to Reality*, 21.
21. Lewis, *Pilgrim's Regress*, 48.
22. Lewis, *Pilgrim's Regress*, 61.

Whether it's reduction all the way down to subatomic particles, or just down to lumps of organic material, the imperium of
scientism assaults both our common sense and our values—de-
manding we assent to its vision of the world as "all other than it
is." If we are told that being in love is just a bunch of chemicals
(testosterone, dopamine, oxytocin, etc.), we should find this as
nonsensical as the claim that the game of chess is just a bunch of
plastic and cardboard. In each case, the claim mistakes the material basis (or "material cause," as the Aristotelians say) of a thing
for the thing itself. A chessboard is made of cardboard, and chess
pieces made of plastic, but cardboard and plastic are not what
chess is. Likewise, there is a biochemical basis of being in love,
but the chemicals are not the thing itself that is being in love. Being in love essentially involves thoughts about another person and
about oneself in relation to that person. An account of love that
makes no room for these features is, for that reason alone, a false
account of love. So, too, in general, an account of what we are
that asserts an identity between us and our material cause leaves
out essential features of what we are and so is false.

If an overconfidence in science skews toward the identification of the human person with his or her body, an overconfidence
in the self-creative power of the individual skews toward a radical separation of the person from his or her embodied humanity.
What we need is something that splits the difference: an understanding of what we are that takes our embodiment seriously—
indeed as essential to what we are—but allows that we are more
than bodies, or animals, or particles.

ABANDON HOPE

Given our contemporary confusion about identity, it is good to
look to the wisdom of the past. Considered as a personification,
Lady Philosophy is the spokeswoman for the whole wisdom

34

tradition of Western philosophy. Boethius had long ago been initiated into that tradition—he is a citizen of the imperishable city—but in his bad state he must be reminded. Lady Philosophy's first diagnosis was that Boethius had forgotten who he was, identifying himself with those things outside himself on which he had staked his happiness. But she senses there is a deeper sickness still, and it too has to do with identity. She begins to question him about the whence and the whither of the cosmos, but also about himself: "Do you remember that you are a man?" Of course, he replies. "I am a mortal, rational animal" (*rationale animal atque mortale*) (C 1.6p, 28).

To a philosopher in the classical tradition, this should be a perfectly acceptable answer. It could almost be described as a paraphrase of Epictetus (writing in Greek): "'What is a human being?' 'A rational, mortal creature.'"[23] Long before, Aristotle had characterized the human being as like other animals with respect to our metabolic and sensory powers and our mortality, with the peculiar distinction of being rational.[24]

But Lady Philosophy is dissatisfied. "Is there nothing more you can add?" "Nothing," he says (C 1.6p, 28).

We might wonder what more there could be. Isn't our rationality that noblest part of us that keeps us above the beasts? But in Lady Philosophy's judgment there is something more, and more noble, about what we are. Boethius's ignorance of this something more is his deepest problem: "Now I know," she concludes, "the other, in fact the greatest, cause of your disease: you no longer know what you are" (C 1.6p, 28).

So, what are we? She doesn't say! Not yet anyway. But we can foreshadow a bit. Lady Philosophy does not tell Boethius his answer is wrong. She agrees with him that a human being is a mortal rational animal. The problem is Boethius's ignorance about the

---

23. Epictetus, *Discourses* 2.9.1–2, in *The Complete Works*, trans. Waterfield, 158.
24. Aristotle, *Nicomachean Ethics* 1.7 1098a.

"something more." Eventually, she will show him in what way he is more than a mortal rational animal—see the end of chapter 6 if you are impatient. In doing so, she will also show us how to split the difference between the inadequate accounts of human nature bequeathed to us by the competing reigns of individualism and of scientism.

Against the scientistic outlook, Lady Philosophy will contend that we are more than animals. But against the individualistic outlook, she will hold that we are indeed animals—of a special sort, to be sure, but animals nonetheless. We need to come to grips with our mortality and our physicality in order to arrive at wisdom about what can and cannot make us truly happy. The maxim "Know thyself," as it is often observed, was not an invitation to introspect about your preferences or personality type but instead an injunction to recognize your limits. Don't be like Icarus, whose fake wings made him think he could fly to the sun. "You are a toy!" Woody tells Buzz Lightyear—and only then is Buzz able to do any good.

At the same time, we find ourselves with this hardly bearable longing to be more than a toy, to have real wings. This restlessness is deeply rooted in our psychology. It causes wishful thinking. It causes delusions of grandeur. But it also causes us to innovate, to ease the burden of being animals. Toilet paper and sewer systems make being animals less gross. Insulation and HVAC make it less uncomfortable and more stable to live in a world of seasons. Medicine not only prolongs life but makes it less painful. Cars and airplanes lift the limitations of distance. Music, painting, sculpture, and other arts and crafts defy the Marxist lie that material welfare is all that matters to us. The universality of religious belief and practice attest to a hope not only in some realm beyond nature but in the possibility that we might participate in it. There is therefore a kernel of wisdom in the idea that what we are is up to us to choose: we are not altogether bound by our biology or our physicality. This hints at the "something more" that Boethius could not offer, and that confirmed Lady Philosophy's second diagnosis that he had forgotten what he is.

But instead of telling Boethius straightaway what he is, she tells him to give up hope (C 1.7m). The most famous literary command to give up hope is written on the gates of Dante's hell: "Abandon all hope you who enter here."[25] Now, I am no doctor (the kind that can help people), and I have never been to medical school. But telling the patient to give up hope does not seem like an example of good bedside manner. Doctor: "Ah, now I know what is wrong with you." Patient: "Ok, tell it to me straight, Doc." Doctor: "It's hopeless."

But while Lady Philosophy is not always nice (remember the Muses), she has what we need. Hope is one of the three great virtues of the Christian tradition, but it is possible to hope for the wrong things. In this respect, hope is like faith. It is a sort of proverb that you just have to have faith. But if your faith is mere credulity, or an ignorant trust in what is impossible or unreal, then you shouldn't have faith. So, too, with hope: if your hope is for things you really cannot have, or wouldn't be good for you if you could have them, you should abandon that hope. "Wait without hope, for hope would be hope for the wrong things,"[26] the poet counsels sick souls.

It might seem calloused, but the prescription to give up is part of Lady Philosophy's therapy. One of Heraclitus's fragments says that the way up and the way down are one and the same. As with all of Heraclitus's fragments, we do not know what he meant. But he has been interpreted to mean that in order to go up, we must first go down. An honest effort, at sobriety, nirvana, mystical union with God, or even simply coping with the challenge of living, must begin with a recognition of just how screwed up we

25. Dante, *Inferno* 3.9, trans. Esolen, 23.
26. Eliot, "East Coker" 3, *Four Quartets*, 28.

really are. And what is screwy about your life is not merely your circumstances, the messed up things that God or the universe or other people have thrown your way, but *you yourself*. Your selfishness, bitterness, pettiness, vindictiveness, vain ambitions, meager desires. To progress, you must let go of these. No medicine, no therapy, will bring healing unless you stop clinging to false hopes.

This is the wisdom of those ancient philosophers who lived without hope but tried to live well. Dante honors them by placing them in the least unpleasant circle of hell.[27] Understanding our vulnerability as humans, including the overarching vulnerability of our mortality, Stoic wisdom warns us of the dangers of hope. Hope stokes desire, makes us restless, and is at odds with the effort to stake your chance for happiness only on what is in your control.

But what if hope could be shown to be well-grounded in reason—not a fool's hope? Then, even if living in hope proved difficult, or even if achieving the object of hope were not guaranteed, it might be worth it after all. Lady Philosophy's prescription to give up hope is bitter, but sweet. Speaking of Boethius's unforeseen downfall, she advises: "Suppose this very fickleness [of fortune] is for you a source of hope for better things" (C 2.2p, 37).

27. Dante, *Inferno* 4.

3

Goods of Fortune

OUT OF CONTROL

Zeno of Citium has been hailed as the founding father of Stoicism.[1] But before he settled down as a philosopher, he was a merchant. Sailing from somewhere in Phoenicia to Piraeus, the port city of Athens, poor Zeno was shipwrecked, losing a cargo of purple cloth. Somehow, he made it to shore, and in his downtime started reading *Memorabilia* by Xenophon (430–354 BC), a book of philosophical dialogues starring Plato's teacher Socrates. Inspired to adopt a philosophical life, Zeno apprenticed himself to the first philosopher he met, a man named Crates (365–285).

This Crates had been a disciple of Diogenes of Sinope (404–323 BC), the great Cynic. But the Cynics had little more to offer than a sort of needle with which to prick the balloon of men's vanity—including their own, it should be said in fairness. No one in Greece had a sharper wit or enjoyed his life less than Diogenes. A biographer reports that his best friends were convinced he had committed suicide.[2]

For as long as men are mortal, and for as long as men do wicked things, the Cynics will always attract followers. This is because death and wickedness tempt everyone to despair from time to time, and Cynicism is the philosophy of despair—though

---

1. Diogenes Laertius, "Life of Zeno" 32, in *Lives* 7.
2. Diogenes Laertius, "Life of Diogenes" 11, in *Lives* 6.

not so desperate as the contemporary movement known as anti-natalism, one prominent advocate of which argues, and claims to believe, that it is harmful to exist and so it would have been better for *everyone*, no matter how much you enjoy your life, never to have been born.[3] Ah, progress.

It is to Zeno's credit that he moved past the despair of his teacher. Men are mortal, men do wicked things, but men *can be* virtuous, and virtue is a protection—not a protection against death but against many of our vulnerabilities. In his efforts to move past his cynical teachers, Zeno began to recover one of Plato's central insights, itself probably gleaned from his teacher Socrates: that the virtuous life is the happy life,[4] *come what may.* Eventually, he would look back at his lost fortune of purple cloth and say, "I now find that I made a prosperous voyage when I was wrecked."[5]

This is an application of one of the great reframing techniques of Stoic ethics. Losing a shipload of cargo to the sea, when you make a living as a merchant, sure looks like a bad thing. But the startling Stoic conviction is that it can be a good thing, if you let it be. "People are troubled not by things but by their judgments of things," Epictetus says.[6] "There is no situation miserable unless you think it so," Lady Philosophy tells Boethius (C 2.4p, 43).

Having diagnosed Boethius's illness, Lady Philosophy's first round of treatment is to remind him how little control he has over the things he has come to mistake as his own. There are these various attractive things, call them *goods of fortune*. Lady Philosophy's goal here is two-fold: She wants to convince Boethius, first, that he has little to no control over the goods of fortune, and second, that no good of fortune or combination thereof can make him happy. She will then be ready to deliver the very good news

3. Benatar, *Better Never to Have Been*, 19–59.
4. Plato, *Republic* 1 353d–354a.
5. Diogenes Laertius, "Life of Zeno" 5, in *Lives* 7, trans. Yonge, 260.
6. Epictetus, *Handbook* 5a, in *The Complete Works*, trans. Waterfield, 47.

that *something* can make him happy and that it is partially within his control.

In her efforts to disabuse Boethius of the belief that happiness depends on goods of fortune, Lady Philosophy proceeds, at first, not strictly *philosophically* but *rhetorically*. "It is not yet time for stronger remedies," she says (C 1.6p, 29). He's not yet ready for philosophy. "Let me apply the sweet persuasion of rhetoric" (C 2.1p, 32). Rhetoric, on its best behavior, so to speak, is in harmony with philosophy. But rhetoric's goal is persuasion. By starting with the medicine of rhetoric, then, Lady Philosophy is allowing for a form of discourse that has somewhat different standards from her own. In particular, rhetoric is free to exaggerate.

But we must remember that it is Lady Philosophy herself who is administering the medicine of rhetoric—she doesn't holler for one of the Muses to come back. And one of the things that Lady Philosophy does, in this mode, is to say something stronger about the goods of fortune than she really means, or than is really the case.[7] Fortune, she tells Boethius, "is not responsible for anything of beauty that you have ever had or lost." Fortune can offer only "counterfeit happiness" (C 2.1p, 31–32). And yet, as becomes clear, Fortune is responsible for such goods as his great wealth (which made the glass and ivory library affordable), his good health, and his successful career through which he gained both influence and prestige. On the surface, isn't there something genuinely good about these things, even if they can't bring perfect happiness and even if they are not fully under our control?

Our answer, I think, is yes. And Lady Philosophy's is too: each of the genuine goods of fortune can contribute in some small way to a happy life. In this respect, they can image or reflect true happiness and—in their proper place—direct our attention not to themselves but to the true beatitude they reflect.

7. Marenbon, *Boethius*, 103.

Lady Philosophy therefore offers a less bleak description of our relationship to the goods of fortune than the Stoics did. On their view, every good of fortune should be a matter of indifference. But as the anthologist Stobaeus put it, some of these are "preferred" while others are "dispreferred." All else being equal, it is rational to prefer the preferred indifferents.[8] Yet according to Seneca, there is "no real good" in the goods of fortune: "I have always found they were empty and, though painted over with showy and deceptive colours, have nothing within to match their outward show."[9]

Boethius's departure from the Stoics about the value of goods of fortune doubtless stems from his belief that goodness and being are "convertible": everything that exists, he thinks, just insofar as it exists, is good. Just why he thinks this, and how he reconciles this with the reality of evil, we will consider later, in chapter 7. For now, it is enough to note that given the conviction that everything that exists is good, Boethius can't follow the Stoics in holding every good of fortune to be indifferent. It is permissible to want these things because they really are good. But their goodness is quite limited compared to the sort of goodness our hearts yearn for. When we mistake any one of these goods of fortune for that supreme goodness we yearn for, and pursue the former as though it were the latter, heartbreak is inevitable.

We must not cling to the goods of fortune. "He who binds to himself a joy / Does the winged life destroy / He who kisses the joy as it flies / Lives in eternity's sunrise."[10] Initiation into the secret of true happiness requires distinguishing the joys that flit and fly from the solid rock we can build a life on.

We all basically know that the goods of fortune cannot make us truly happy. But most of us think this not because we perceive

---

8. Stobaeus 2.84–85, in Long and Sedley, *Hellenistic Philosophers* 58E, 1:355.

9. Seneca, *De Consolatione ad Helviam* 5.426–29, trans. in Herold, "Boethius's *Consolatio Philosophiae* as a Bridge," 19.

10. Blake, "Eternity," in *Poems*, 94.

the inadequacy of these goods but instead because life forces us to recognize that these goods are outside our control. We know we can't hold on to them. But if we could . . .

The really deep thing going on in Boethius's critique of the goods of fortune is his insistence that these things cannot make us truly happy *not only* because we can't hold on to them *but also* because they do not have the right sort of nature to make us truly happy. Thus, even if we could hold on to them, even if we were as well-endowed as a man can be, still they could not make us happy. There is an alignment between the kind of thing that can make us truly happy and the kind of thing we can hold on to, an alignment that begins to emerge as nothing short of providential. But we are still a long way from that.

WHEEL OF FORTUNE

To cure Boethius of his attachment to goods of fortune, Lady Philosophy invents a *dramatis persona*, Lady Fortune, a character fictional both in the story world and in our own. Plato used a similar technique in *Crito*, in which the character Socrates has the Laws of Athens speak. By portraying them sympathetically as stern but compassionate and fragile, Socrates makes the prospect of his unlawful escape from prison less attractive.[11] By making Lady Fortune not exactly villainous but untrustworthy and not very likable, Lady Philosophy makes the goods she represents less attractive. Or that at least is the rhetorical strategy.

Lady Fortune is depicted with her famous wheel. Like the contestants in the eponymous gameshow long hosted by Pat Sajak and Vanna White, the wheel goes round and—*ding ding*—it lands on a shiny wedge and you get a thousand dollars for every letter you turn over. Now spin it again, with the same force and determination, and it lands on the bankrupt wedge that takes

11. Plato, *Crito* 50a–54e.

all your earnings away. For everything subject to the Wheel of Fortune, your own efforts do not ultimately matter. You can do everything right and the wheel can give you precisely the opposite of what you'd hoped for; you can do everything wrong and get exactly what you'd hoped for. Fortune and her wheel are fickle like that.

The figure of the Wheel of Fortune is not comfortless. There once was a boy named Eustace Clarence Scrubb, and he almost deserved it. He goes on an adventure at sea unwillingly and antagonizes everyone, even those who mean him well. Eventually, he is transformed into a dragon, and in his dragonish condition begins to repent from his obnoxious ways and longs to be human again and have real friendships. But his mere wishing it won't remove his dragon scales. Sir Reepicheep the Mouse, whom Eustace had badly abused, is compassionate toward him. He visits him and offers words of comfort, telling him about knights and ladies and kings and other illustrious persons who had taken their own sorrowful turns on the Wheel of Fortune.[12] He does not tell him that the wheel eventually turned round in their favor. Reepicheep's comfort strategy seems to have been this: noble men and women have experienced the same sort of thing you are now experiencing, Eustace; you, too, can suffer nobly, as they did.

But what sorts of goods, exactly, are supposed to be within Lady Fortune's control? She describes herself like an elemental force of nature. The heavens control weather; the solar year controls seasons; the sea is now placid, now raging. These have their rights; shall she be denied hers? But Fortune is not philosophically precise, and neither should we expect her to be. Despite her attribution of weather and seasons to other forces of nature, just a few lines later she claims responsibility for a rainstorm that put out the flames of a funeral pyre (C 2.2p).

---

12. Lewis, *Voyage of the Dawn Treader*, in *Chronicles of Narnia*, 472.

The kinds of goods under her control only emerge after her exit, when Lady Philosophy explains what they are. In the most general sense, these goods are those we can lose even if we are perfectly wise, courageous, temperate, and just. These four cardinal virtues may tend to make their possessors better off with respect to the goods of fortune than those who lack them; but there is no necessary connection between being either perfectly virtuous or perfectly vicious and having or failing to have these goods.

Under this most general category of goods that we can fail to have even if we are perfectly virtuous, Boethius follows a classical tradition stretching back to Aristotle (and implicitly Plato) in distinguishing four subcategories: sensual pleasure, wealth, prestige, and power. We might think that in an ideal world, there would be a strict correlation between enjoying these goods and possessing the virtues. But there is not. So Lady Philosophy's heuristic device (at this stage in Boethius's treatment) is Lady Fortune: a fickle goddess who distributes her goods in a way that from our point of view is more or less random.

That is what Reepicheep seems to have recognized: Eustace had been a nuisance, but he should not interpret his dragonish condition as having a law-like correlation with his bad behavior. After all, even if he deserved it, plenty of comparably annoying boys do not get turned into dragons. Reepicheep wants Eustace to bear his suffering with fortitude, so that it might ennoble him.

The degree of attachment to these four categories of fortune's goods—pleasure, wealth, prestige, power—varies from person to person. Lady Philosophy has something to offer each of us. For each category, she shows us both that it is the sort of good that is subject to Fortune and so can be taken from us against our will despite our best efforts, and also that it is not the sort of good that can make us truly happy, anyway.

So there is something truly bittersweet here. The bitter: these good things we are so attached to are not really within our control. But the sweet: we shouldn't be so attached to them anyway because they cannot give us what we really want. Following Lady Philosophy's instructions is therefore liberating, however uncomfortable it might feel at first.

In *Consolation*, Lady Fortune really is an agent of chaos, and it is not clear how there can be room for her in Boethius's orderly cosmology. But remember, Lady Philosophy introduces Fortune as a heuristic device, or, to return to the medical metaphor, as a part of her sweet and gentle remedy of Rhetoric, preparing Boethius for stronger medicine to come. It seems to me that in a later vignette of Lady Fortune, we meet a Fortune at home in a well-ordered cosmos. In Dante's (1265–1321) *Inferno*, written about eight hundred years after *Consolation* and very much under its influence, Lady Fortune is still up to her old tricks; she is "a general minister and guide / To scramble now and then the empty goods / from race to race, from one blood to another, / past all defense man's shrewdness might devise." But here, she turns her wheel as the delegated agent of a higher authority. She is a wise angel who "sees / ahead, she judges, and she follows through / in her realm."[13]

Her depiction in *Inferno*—*nota bene*, she is not depicted as a resident in Hell; rather, Virgil teaches Dante about her as these two are traveling through Hell—suggests that Fortune is no longer simply a figure against whom we must guard ourselves by detaching our desires from the goods in her control. Now she is heaven-sent, still unpredictable but deputized for our benefit to keep us hopeful for something greater than the goods she can bestow and withdraw. You'd almost be tempted to think that Dante the poet had read *Consolation* all the way to the end.

13. Dante, *Inferno* 7.73–96, trans. Esolen, 69–71.

PLEASURE

At almost exactly the same time as Zeno's first lectures in the Stoa, a philosopher named Epicurus (341–270 BC) bought a piece of land in Athens called simply the Garden. At the Garden, he shared his own philosophy with any who would listen. For his basic convictions about the fundamental nature of reality, Epicurus drew on the original Greek atomists, Leucippus (fifth century BC) and Democritus (460–370 BC). Atomism holds that the bodies of our ordinary experience are composed of very tiny, indivisible particles—the Greek word *atomos* simply means "without division." Epicurus's atomism extends to human souls as well: our souls no less than our bodies are composed of atoms. For Epicurus, the whole really is just the sum of its parts.

The literary scholar Stephen Greenblatt, perhaps the most well-known contemporary advocate of the Epicurean worldview, recognized its affinity with the reductive mechanistic worldview forged during the "scientific revolution" of the sixteenth century.[14] But to avoid the determinism that atomism suggests—and which would make it a matter of pure luck who experiences pleasure and who pain—Epicurus introduced, and his later follower Lucretius (99–55 BC) developed, the concept of "the swerve." A swerve is a random deviation in atomic motion.[15] Each swerve makes it so that the subsequent course of the universe is not completely determined by its causal past; likewise, future swerves make it impossible to predict the future. Through the swerve, the Epicureans hoped to leave a little room for free will.

Whether or not it really can leave room for free will, this total atomism about the human person fits nicely with Epicurus's fundamental conviction about ethics: that pleasure is the only good and pain the only evil. We are to imagine feelings of pleasure and pain arising more or less mechanistically (barring a swerve) as a

14. Greenblatt, *The Swerve*, 6.
15. McKirahan, *Philosophy Before Socrates*, 342; Lucretius, *On the Nature of Things* 2.216–93.

purely bodily reaction to contact and pressure from surrounding bodies. The good life is the life of pleasure and the bad life a life of pain.

Epicureanism is sometimes unfairly conflated with a similar philosophy known as hedonism. Both hedonism and Epicureanism hold that only pleasure is good. But hedonism as it is typically understood does not discriminate between higher and lower pleasures: the thing to do here and now is whatever strikes you as most pleasant; so if that extra slice of pizza would taste really good, you should eat it. By contrast, Epicureanism is more prudent: gorging yourself on pizza might feel good in the moment, but your ensuing tummyache, obesity, and high cholesterol will likely cause much more pain in the long run than a habit of overeating pizza will bring pleasure.

Epicureanism also distinguishes between types of pleasures. Lower pleasures, such as those arising from the enjoyment of food and drink and sex, are the kind of pleasures that are inextricable from pain—arguably, the pleasure of these activities is little more than a relief from the pain of desire. Pursuing this sort of pleasure, then, involves being in constant pain.[16] The wisdom of Epicurus is that through the virtues, we can detach ourselves from these lower pleasures and be less violently disturbed by our appetites. Experiencing less pain will correspondingly reduce our urge to get pleasure through the satisfaction of these appetites.

So then in what sense is pleasure the good, for the Epicureans? "The removal of all pain is the limit of the magnitude of pleasures," he is reported to have taught."[17] In Cicero's *De finibus* (*On Ends*), the character Torquatus, spokesman for Epicureanism, says this: "The greatest pleasure according to us is that which is experienced as a result of the complete removal of pain."[18] The

16. Epicurus, "Letter to Menoeceus," in Long and Sedley, *Hellenistic Philosophers* 21B, 1:113–14.

17. Epicurus, *Key Doctrines* 3, in Long and Sedley, *Hellenistic Philosophers* 21C, 1:115.

18. Cicero, *De finibus* 1.11, trans. Rackham, 41.

Epicurean ideal is in fact something very close to, if not indistin-
guishable from, the Stoic goal of tranquility (*ataraxia*).[19]

Epicureanism is therefore also like Stoicism in setting its aim
for human beings too low. We want something more than the
absence of pain—something positive, not negative. But Epicureanism sets its aim far lower than Stoicism. Stoics and Epicureans
concur that no one achieves tranquility without virtue. But the
Stoics made virtue the highest good—the thing chosen for its
own sake. The Epicureans by contrast make pleasure the highest
good: they recognize that virtue grants the highest pleasure and
so pursue virtue *for the sake of* pleasure. As Torquatus asks rhetorically, "were [the virtues] not productive of pleasure, who would
deem them either praiseworthy or desirable?"[20]

No wonder, then, that Cicero dismisses the Epicurean em-
phasis on pleasure as "a doctrine in the last degree unworthy of
the dignity of man." Nature, he continues, "has created and endowed us for higher ends."[21] Indeed, it is hard to explain Cicero's own courageous speeches defending the ideal of the Republic
against looming tyranny, speeches which led to his brutal assassination by decapitation,[22] on the backward Epicurean assumption
that virtue is only worth pursuing for pleasure's sake. Generaliz-
ing from Cicero's example, it seems obvious that life confronts
us with many situations in which we have the option to pursue
pleasure or to do something else that is not pleasant but that we
judge to be the better thing to do. Even if we take into account
Epicurus's focus on high pleasures, including (in his mind) the
highest of all, tranquility, still it happens that sometimes we act
in a way that has nothing to do with the pursuit of pleasure and
everything to do with the pursuit of what is right, or noble, or

19. Long and Sedley, *Hellenistic Philosophers*, 1:124.
20. Cicero, *De finibus* 1.13, trans. Rackham, 47.
21. Cicero, *De finibus* 1.7, trans. Rackham, 25.
22. Plutarch, *Cicero* 48, in *Lives*, 7:207.

beautiful, or loving. Circumstances like these make it obvious that, however good pleasure might be, it is not the highest good.

And it's a good thing that it is not the highest good, because pleasure is one of those types of good that is subject to fortune and so is outside our control. We are not ultimately in control of how much pleasure we can experience in life—even a virus like COVID-19 can rob us of the pleasure of tasty foods. Sensual pleasures in general obviously are subject to the fortunes of sickness, injury, and disease, not to mention time itself and so old age and death. Moreover, we all know from experience that there are things we judge to be more worth our pursuit than pleasure—even and perhaps especially in those circumstances where we choose the pleasant knowing that the unpleasant is the better option. Noble Cicero did not shun aristocratic delicacies, but knew when fortune had forced him into a choice between what is pleasant and what is right.

Lady Philosophy considers Epicurus's pleasure-first mentality beneath "the study of men," hardly worthy of refutation (C 3.2p, 68). "If bodily pleasures could make men become blessed, there is no reason why we shouldn't call cattle blessed, since the aims of these beasts are entirely directed to fulfilling their bodily wants" (C 3.7p, 78–79).

At the same time, she recognizes that of all the imperfect goods that we humans mistake as the ultimate good, more pursue pleasure in this way than any other type of good (C 3.2p). I can attest, as a teacher, that many of my students think it is simply obvious that pleasure is the highest good. Even when students are reasonably serious about morality, they tend to think of morality as a set of rules about the ways in which pleasure ought not to be pursued, rather than a wholesome constituent of a life oriented toward something more important, and more desirable, than pleasure.

There is nothing in Boethius remotely to suggest that pleasure is not good; his point instead is that it is not our highest good. In fact, he seems to accord pleasure a slightly more important role in the ideally happy life than his great medieval successor, Thomas Aquinas (1224–1274). For Aquinas, pleasure is not the highest good, but someone who has attained the highest good experiences pleasure as a result, or "proper accident," of that attainment.[23] But Boethius holds that those who orient their lives around the pursuit of pleasure really are pursuing some genuine *component* of an ideally happy life, however misguidedly, rather than something that is merely a *consequence* of the happy life (C 3.2p).

WEALTH

When it comes to pleasure, many people really do think it is the best thing, and need to be shown that it is not. Comparatively few would affirm that wealth and what money can buy are the highest goods. Yet many live functionally as though they are. It is so difficult for so many of us not to pine for more money, ordering our lives around the pursuit of it.

As with every type of good of fortune, the problem with money is two-fold: it is subject to fortune and so not entirely in our control, and even if it were in our control, it would not make us happy anyway. Remember Zeno's shipwreck: the lost wealth represented by all that purple cloth was in the end good for Zeno because it freed him from attachment to wealth. Seneca counsels us to "bear in mind how much lighter is the pain of not having money than of losing it."[24]

However little or much we do have of wealth and possessions, we don't have full control over these, we are robbed of our delight in them by the labor and worry it takes to hold on to them, and

---

23. Aquinas, *Summa theologiae* 1-2.2.6, trans. Williams, in *Basic Works*, 335.
24. Seneca, *On Tranquility of Mind*, trans. Costa, 85.

eventually we all recognize, however reluctantly, maybe only near death, that they either are not what we esteem, or are not what we should esteem, as worthy of our highest aspirations. It is always instructive to be reminded that at the time of their deaths, people hardly ever express regret about not having made as much money or accumulated as many things as they had wished for; at the end of their lives people value their personal relationships above all.[25]

The wealthy go to great lengths to preserve their wealth, hiring advisors and accountants and lawyers at great expense to avoid the calamity of losing money. Those with many possessions experience both the delight of making use of them but also the anxiety of losing them. "Men who possess very many things need very many things" (C 2.5p, 48). More to lose, more to fear. Many dream of being rich enough to live behind bars in a gated community, preferably with a manned gatehouse: "The riches that were thought to make man self-sufficient instead cause him to need some outside protection" (C 3.3p, 71). Thus, money and possessions cannot make us as happy as we feel that they should make us, because of both the labor we must devote to protect them, and the fear we might lose them anyway.

If only I'd bought a thousand Bitcoins in 2011! If only there weren't burglars or hurricanes! If only there weren't such things as moths and oxidization! I once bought a Merino wool sweater at a department store in Oxford that for nearly twenty years stayed remarkably, almost miraculously, free of pilling. But even this immaculate garment finally succumbed, only last year, to the moth's tooth: it is now pitifully riddled with holes, a reluctant testimony to the evanescence even of our most stalwart possessions. My beloved Gertie, a 1994 Toyota Land Cruiser, who spent long years in the San Juan Mountains of Colorado, laments her spots of rust and her crumbling quarter panels. She holds on—Sturdy Gertie, Perdy Gertie, Dirty Gertie, as we call her—but Father Time will

25. Waldinger and Schulz, *The Good Life*, 28–49.

take back his own. What a pathetic form of life I would lead if my hopes for happiness were dashed by my empty Bitcoin wallet or my decaying sweater and truck.

But there is a deeper reason these can't make us truly happy: they do not have the right sort of nature to do so. Any amount of wealth you can acquire, anything money can buy: these are less valuable than you yourself are. These things are beneath you in dignity. The sort of thing most worth pursuing must be at least as good as we ourselves are. Pursuing things like dollars and cars and houses and watches and diamonds, as though these were the things most worth pursuing in life, debases a human being. People like that are like hogs digging for truffles—nothing wrong with the truffles, but brutish to structure one's life around their acquisition. In attaching ourselves to these material goods, we become their servants—precisely the opposite of how it should be. The human race surpasses "all other earthly creatures," yet "you have thrust your dignity beneath the lowest of things" (C 2.5p, 49).

Boethius will later argue that if there is something that can make a human being truly happy, it must be superior to human beings, such that in our all-in pursuit of it, we do not debase but ennoble ourselves. And this superior thing must be, and must be recognized as, something more than an abstract system of laws or principles, like moral duties. These may well be superior to us, but duty without attraction is alienating. The highest good must be that superior thing we really long for, not just something that makes demands on us.

Boethius's method of evaluation here deserves a little comment, even at the risk of pedantry. It seems to have come naturally for him, in a way it does not for us, to rank things in general according to their goodness or nobility. Humans aren't quite at the top of this hierarchy, but we're pretty high up. Money and the things money can buy are pretty far down the hierarchy. Actions that involve using or making or pursuing things lower than ourselves in the hierarchy of goodness are less good than actions involving things equal or superior to ourselves. This explains in part why we instinctively know—despite our frequent failure to live up to the ideal—that time spent with family and friends (quality time, as we call it) is more valuable than time spent at work or shopping or even playing with toys. It's because people are more valuable than inanimate things. Boethius's judgment that human happiness cannot be found in money or the things money can buy is therefore rooted in this deep recognition that the goodness of things is something out there, in things; it's not in the eye of the beholder. How good a diamond is, and how good your daughter is, are there for you to recognize, not to determine. And if your vision is clear, of course you'll see how far your daughter surpasses the diamond in goodness, and act accordingly.

This Boethian idea of the hierarchy of goodness is not original to Boethius, and we'll discuss some of its antecedents in chapter 6. But for now, notice how it opens up its own distinctive approach to ethical matters: the moral life in large part consists of right recognition of goodness and right action in response to that goodness. Better things deserve more attention than less good things. It is fine to be an entomologist by hobby or profession, but not fine to love bugs more than people—precisely because people are better than bugs. The moral life, on the Boethian view, does not consist in figuring out your preferences (or your community's) and then striving to act in a way consistent with those preferences. It does not consist in trying to maximize pleasure and minimize pain—neither your own nor in general—at every turn. Nor does it really have much to do with figuring out what some moral laws might tell us are our duties and then going about trying to fulfill them. To be in a Boethian world is to be surrounded by goodness, from the lowest low to the highest high, and in that dazzling array, love and enjoy and act on behalf of each good thing we experience in a manner proportionate to its goodness. But we're getting ahead of ourselves.

PRESTIGE, POWER, AND OTHER PEOPLE

We must first speak of the remaining goods of fortune from which Lady Philosophy is trying to liberate Boethius the prisoner: prestige and power. By now, her therapeutic method should be familiar: she shows that these types of goods cannot make us truly happy, and this for two reasons. First, subject to fortune, our enjoyment of them is insecure; second, even if they weren't subject to fortune and so could be securely enjoyed, they do not have the right sort of nature, on their own, to make us truly happy.

In our dealings with other people, at our best and at our worst, we recognize we're dealing with something special—not merely things or feelings but people. It is a high responsibility, or opportunity, to walk amongst our fellow men, as Jacob Marley told Scrooge.[26] In a mysterious way, we tend to judge our own worth as persons by how we measure up to those around us. We long for status, and we long for influence, and these are often hard to disentangle.

Our longing for status is often innocently enough a desire for others to think well of us—to think we are affable, or trustworthy, or cool. But sometimes we want others to think of us as clever, or impressive, or even intimidating—or at least some of us do. In these latter cases it's hard to disentangle the longing for status among other people from a desire for power over other people. This desire for power might be no worse (and no better) than a desire not to be hurt by others—to protect oneself. But we know all too well, from history or autobiography as the case may be, that this same desire might manifest as a desire to dominate or hurt other people. St. Augustine of Hippo (354–430) warns

26. Dickens, *A Christmas Carol*, 47.

us against this desire; Nietzsche urges those who have ears to hear
to embrace it.

Lady Philosophy offers a cold shower to this *libido dom-
inandi*—this lust for power. Our status among other people is
not fully within our control. Haters gonna hate, as they say. You
can try to do everything right and still be vulnerable to snub or
insult or cancellation. You can sacrifice all your convictions and
integrity trying to please others and get nothing in return, not
even Wales.[27] You can flex like a Viking and still pull a hamstring.
For that matter, you can be completely successful like Alexander
and conquer the known world, then sit down and cry for the infinite other worlds that cannot be conquered.[28] Other people, as a
group, are in reality finite in number but for all practical purposes
innumerable: there is no end to the effort to please or control all
of them. Other people, as individuals, are infinite in the sense
that they are ultimately unfathomable. You might trick yourself
into believing you have those around you figured out, only to be
surprised by new or hitherto undisclosed beliefs or preferences, or
changes in their own fortunes or character. It is perilous to stake
your hope for happiness on the good opinion of other people or
on your chances of controlling them.

Boethius was an aristocrat, and a politician, used to power
and the esteem of high office and high learning. Despite his com-
plaints about his faded beauty, or the loss of his fancy library,
what seems to have bothered him most is the shame of being
cast out of high society (C 3.4p). If you are, like me, unused to
high society, this shame might seem shallow. But it is not hard to
generalize to other contexts: there are pecking orders in the public
school playground and on the job site no less than in the senate.
The fact is that most of us, even when our moral convictions are a
bit lax, are not willing to violate norms egregiously to gain more

27. Bolt, *Man for All Seasons*, 158.
28. Plutarch, "On Tranquility of Mind" 4 466D, in *Moralia*, 6:177.

pleasure and wealth and possessions. We tend not to want to be shunned by our fellows, even when violation of norms offers a clear path to material gain. Of course, there are exceptions. The point is that, regardless of economic class or profession, desires for prestige and power run deep.

And rightly so, it must be said. These desires are a sign of our longing to belong to a community and have a real role to play in the welfare of that community. Like any desires, they can become corrupted. But the desire for status and influence, prestige and power, is not itself corrupt.

One of the ways it becomes corrupted is when either prestige or power or both are taken to be the highest good—the things worth pursuing above all other things. And it is for this corrupted desire that Lady Philosophy's medicine is so effective: you cannot perfectly curate others' perceptions of you, and you cannot control everything about everyone, so the Alexanders and Napoleons of the world are bound to fail. But even if you could have it all under control, this would not make you happy: if seven billion people adored you and were under your thumb, you would wish there to be more people. And even those seven billion would be hard to manage: imagine the fear and anxiety of keeping them all in line; even if you outsourced to a PR firm, you'd have to worry about keeping the firm on your side. The tyrant, Plato taught us, is the most fearful of all men.[29] Adam Duritz sang movingly in the Counting Crows song, "Mr. Jones," that "when everybody loves me, / I'm gonna be just about as happy as I can be." But he was wrong.

Yet there is something right in the thought that in our relationships with other people, we are drawing nearer to the sort of goods that really might be our highest good. Boethius was very sensitive to this insight. Friendship is the most sacred good (C 3.2p) he said, probably with a little exaggeration but

29. Plato, *Republic* 9 579e.

still sincerely. Lady Philosophy comforts Boethius with the reminder that while he has indeed suffered Fortune's reversal, he
still enjoys the great blessing of a loving and good family: his admirable father-in-law, "greatest glory of the human race"; chaste
and honorable wife, "worthy as her father"; and illustrious sons,
who "even in youth show evidence of the nature of their father
and grandfather" (C 2.4p, 41). "Even now," Lady Philosophy tells
Boethius, "you have those things that no one can deny are dearer
than life" (C 2.4p, 42).

Boethius's recognition of the great goodness of close relationships represents one of his greatest departures from his Stoic pre-
decessors. The Stoics recognized that other people are among the
things we can lose; therefore, we must exert an effort to achieve
apatheia even with respect to our friends and family. To free his
pupils from their normal human fears about losing loved ones,
Epictetus counseled them to think of their closest relations not as
wife or son but simply as humans: "If you kiss a child of yours or
your wife, tell yourself that you're kissing a human being, because
then you won't be upset if they die."[30] Not that the love of wife or
children is bad. "Once a child is born, it's impossible for us not to
love it and care for it,"[31] he concedes. But don't make too much
of them, just as you shouldn't make too much of a delectable
crustacean or mushroom: "If you have a dear wife or child given
you, they are like the shellfish or the truffle, they are very well in
their way."[32] There is a lot of wisdom in the ethics of detachment.
But here, Epictetus has gone too far.

Remember, for Boethius what is most worth loving is what
is equal or superior to oneself. Tethering our lives to other people
will always keep us vulnerable to Fortune, because while Fortune
is not what makes men mortal, she does have some control over

30. Epictetus, *Handbook* 3, in *The Complete Works*, trans. Waterfield, 46.

31. Epictetus, *Discourses* 1.23.5, in *The Complete Works*, trans. Waterfield, 120.

32. Epictetus, *Manual* 7, trans. Matheson, in Saunders, ed., *Greek and Roman Philosophy
After Aristotle*, 135.

the time and manner of our deaths. But Boethius sees, and even Lady Philosophy agrees, that when it comes to people, this vulnerability is worth it because of the great goodness of people. Even the greatest relationships cannot make us perfectly happy, but that's ok, they were never meant to do that to begin with.

So concludes what we might think of as the (mostly) negative or deconstructive part of Lady Philosophy's therapy: persuading Boethius, first through the rhetoric of Lady Fortune and her wheel and then through philosophical arguments, of the inadequacy of the goods under Fortune's control for making us truly happy. But she wants more for him than simply to believe that the best happiness available to him is the virtuous suffering of the ignominy of exile and imprisonment, and the horror of torture and execution. She wants him to know how virtue makes happiness possible under these conditions, and to know what he can reasonably hope for, on the other side of suffering. In what follows, therefore, we will begin to consider the more positive or reconstructive part of that therapy.

4

On the Good

Sometimes we do bad things on purpose. In his *Confessions*, Augustine tells a story from his wayward youth in which he and his buddies steal a bunch of pears from a neighbor's tree. They did this not because they were hungry, but to be mischievous. It's the sort of mischief countless boys and girls get up to and then grow out of, and for most of us, in hindsight we see our own versions of pear-stealing as bad, but not *that bad*. Yet the mature and reflective Augustine, reflecting on this youthful episode, condemned himself in the strongest possible terms. It seemed to him, as he reflected, that he and his mates not only knew what they were doing was wrong but did it *because* it was wrong. It seems, then, that according to his self-assessment, Augustine did evil for evil's sake.

And this is a profoundly unsettling conclusion. It had been a commonplace of philosophical reflection prior to Augustine that we always and only seek some good in our actions, even our bad actions. Here's an obvious example: it's bad to steal, but you steal not because it's bad but because you're hungry and it's good to eat. Your wrong action in this case is done in pursuit of a genuinely good thing. And the wrongness of the action does not magically negate the goodness of the good thing you were trying to achieve. But Augustine seems to be saying that he and his friends did their bad action for the sake of its badness.

60

Can we make any sense out of this? I'm skeptical. But this is a highly contested topic in the history of philosophy. Some think that if we are truly free, if we truly have free will, it follows that we can will anything for any reason or even no reason. It would then follow that we can will evil for evil's sake, or will evil just because. William of Ockham (1287–1347) is probably the most famous defender of this view that the will's freedom is totally untethered from goodness.

But the major theme about human action in the wisdom tradition of Western philosophy is that we always seek the good, even when we seek it badly. And while Augustine's reflections on the petty wickedness of his pear-theft really is a somber reminder of the way we humans can ally ourselves to darkness, his story also reveals that even here there was still something inside him on the side of the light. For he tells us that he doesn't think he would have stolen the pears without his buddies. There was something about the sociality of the sin—whether camaraderie or plain old peer pressure—that gave the sin a glimmer of goodness.

Boethius is firmly entrenched in this mainstream philosophical tradition that fixes the good as the goal of any action. As a scholar killed in his prime, Boethius's biggest aborted ambition was to translate all of Plato and Aristotle into Latin and "to bring them into harmony and to demonstrate that they do not disagree on everything, as many maintain, but are in the greatest possible agreement on many things that pertain to philosophy."[1]

Perhaps the most important topic on which these founding fathers of philosophy were in agreement was the connection between human action and goodness. "Every action and pursuit is thought to aim at some good; and for this reason the good has rightly been declared to be that at which all things aim."[2] "Every

---

1. Boethius, *Second Commentary on Aristotle's "On Interpretation"* 2, trans. Pelikan, in *The Emergence of Catholic Tradition*, 1:42.

2. Aristotle, *Nicomachean Ethics* 1.1 1094a.

soul pursues the good and does whatever it does for its sake."[3] Boethius (through Lady Philosophy) agrees: "It is the Good that men seek in their various pursuits" (C 3.1p, 67).

The positive pursuit of the good is ubiquitous in human action, not only good actions, not only immoral actions, but even the sort of action that seems mainly palliative, like munching potato chips after a stressful day at work or at home with the kids. To escape from pain is to move closer to the good, even if it is only a timid half step. But at our better moments, we turn to good things seeking something positive rather than escaping something negative. Lady Philosophy's efforts to persuade Boethius not to hope for happiness in any of the goods of fortune—pleasure, wealth, prestige, power—presupposes that he is, and we are, searching *for* something, not just escaping *from* something. If she is right, the takeaway lesson is not that we should pursue no good at all—that is impossible—but that we shouldn't pursue these types of good. Or at least, we should not pursue these as though they are what we are ultimately seeking. In other words, Lady Philosophy's exhortation not to seek the goods of fortune presupposes that we are meant to seek the good.

Of any philosophical thesis, such as the one offered here—that we always seek the good—we may ask not only is it true, but also is it good? That is, assuming its truth, is it good for us? Or, whether or not it is true, is it good for us to believe? Here, I think we have a thesis that is profoundly good for us to believe—in evolutionary terms, belief that we always act for the good is an adaptation conducive to our survival. In our gloomiest moments, or when overwhelmed by our proclivity to evil, the belief that we are hardwired to seek the good is a source of hope that not all is lost.

In general, we cannot infer merely from something's being good for us that it is therefore true or real. If, or when, wishful thinking is irrational, it is so because it fosters the belief that something *is* or

---

3. Plato, *Republic* 6 505e.

will be the case from the fact that we *wish* it to be the case. This is not a good way to live, generally speaking. But when it comes to a belief that we always act for the sake of the good, wishful thinking may well be reasonable. Consider this: right now, either you do in fact pursue the good in everything you do, or you don't. Suppose you do. Then a *belief* that you pursue the good in everything you do is correct. Now suppose you don't. Well, a belief that you pursue the good in everything you do is unhappily false. But there's also this: such a belief will tend to shape your character and your actions. It will be difficult to think of yourself as wicked all through. In moments of self-examination, you will tend to try to identify the good you were aiming at when you did that bad or stupid thing you regret. The belief will help you be a better person. In fact, it will help you become the sort of person who does in fact aim at the good in all you do. Fake it 'til you make it! Sometimes, and perhaps here especially, we become what we believe.

NATURE'S DIRECTION

Suicide is the most important challenge to the thesis that we always seek the good. At his darkest hour in prison, Boethius himself longed to die (C 1.1m). How is it not offensively Pollyannish to go on asserting the old-fashioned doctrine that we always seek the good when there are people out there so overcome by despair that they take their own lives? The answer is that we have no words to offer, either in help or offense, to the dead. We speak to the living. Many of us, in varying degrees of closeness to concrete attempts on our own lives, are acquainted with desires for self-harm. We can think of these as less intense instances of the urge that takes some people all the way to self-destruction, and reason our way to something honest.

For an explanation of this appetite for destruction, some turn to modern sages like Schopenhauer (1788–1860) and Freud

(1856–1939),[4] who have no consolation to offer but whose gloomy diagnoses ring true for people who have been trained to believe that reality is at bottom hostile or indifferent. But those of us on the side of wholesome hope have our own sages. Augustine, for example, defied despair when he explained to his friend Evodius that even the suicidal are seeking the good of peace.[5] They do so irrationally, because peace is not a good they can enjoy, being dead. But they seek peace nonetheless. In doing so, they seek the same peace the saints seek and find in the City of God, "the eternal peace which no adversary can disturb," the "final happiness" and "our last perfection, a consummation which will have no end."[6]

It has been said that what makes drunkenness morally wrong is that it is a kind of little suicide, an intentional depletion of one's highest faculties.[7] And a habit of drunkenness approaches suicide in fact the longer and more entrenched it persists in the life of the drunkard. We might say something similar about certain kinds of drug use, or even the sort of self-inflicted malnutrition of those persistent overeaters of sugar, fat, and salt. Sometimes intemperance is only the tip of an iceberg of immorality.

I mention these examples of overindulgence to show just how common it is for people to do things they know are harmful to themselves. Only in certain extreme instances would we be inclined to describe actions like these as *intentional* self-harm. Such cases are well captured by some songs about drinking, like Bill Anderson and Jon Randall's "Whiskey Lullaby," sung by Alison Krauss and Brad Paisley: "He could never get drunk enough / To get her off his mind until the night / He put that bottle to his head and pulled the trigger / And finally drank away her memory." If I

---

4. Schopenhauer, *World as Will and Representation* 1.4.59; Freud, *Civilization and its Discontents* 5.

5. Augustine, *On Free Choice of the Will* 3.8.

6. Augustine, *City of God* 19.10, trans. Dyson, 932.

7. Ford, *Man Takes a Drink*, 74.

read the song correctly, one night the brokenhearted man intentionally overdosed on alcohol in order to kill himself.

But a similar impulse for harmful excess might also stem from something like a desire to avoid confronting the reality of death and the limitations and responsibility our mortality imposes. Consider Brett and Rennie Sparks's "So Much Wine": "Listen to me, butterfly, there's only so much wine / That you can drink in one life / And it will never be enough / To save you from the bottom of your glass." Here, the bottom of the glass is death or something like death, the death of that melodramatic part of you that wants to maintain an illusion of immortality. Butterfly is going to learn one way or another that our bodies and our responsibility to other people do not permit us to drink forever.

This impulse to do things that are harmful, odd as it sounds and tragic as it is, is ordered to the good. This holds whether or not the self-harmer intentionally aims at self-harm. In the end, there is an important moral difference between self-harming actions that are done in order to harm oneself and those that are not done for that reason but are nevertheless known to be harmful. In the former cases, the self-harm is pursued directly, even if only as a means to something good—release from sorrow, for example, as in "Whiskey Lullaby." In the latter cases, the foreseen self-harm is not directly intended but nevertheless judged worth it in order to get the intended feeling of release or euphoria. And the directly intended self-harm of the former cases makes them morally worse than the latter cases. But here, the point that really matters is that in both sorts of cases, the good is pursued, however defectively.

It remains mysterious why some people harm themselves, even when we can give a plausible story about the good self-harmers seek. We don't need an explanation of why we seek good things, but we would like an explanation of why we sometimes seek the good in self-destructive ways, knowing them to be self-destructive. The mystery might in the end be exactly the same as the unsolvable mystery of free will, original sin, and the inexplicable throwing away of Eden. Maybe it's more like a disease that drugs and therapy can treat or help to mitigate. Of course, it might be both.

I'm convinced there's more to the mystery, however. Think of the good that is pursued in sacrificial action, which by definition is self-harmful. Maximilian Kolbe (1894–1941) was a priest whom the Nazis arrested for his efforts to protect Jews in his native Poland. At Auschwitz, he volunteered to take the place of a fellow prisoner who had been selected, along with nine others, for execution by starvation. For over two weeks, he ministered to his nine companions in death, leading them in prayer. One by one they died until the impatient guards finished off Kolbe and three remaining companions by lethal injection.

Part of what makes Kolbe's action so deeply good is his embrace of a kind of self-harm. Foreseeing the harmful consequences to himself, he acted heroically for another's benefit. He was not directly aiming at his own destruction, but rather the preservation of the man's life, a preservation Kolbe himself could bring about only by giving up his life.

With Kolbe's sacrifice in mind, we can begin to see stupid or immoral examples of self-harm as a sort of corruption of a kind of self-harm that is heroically good to the point of holiness. More generally, in sacrificial actions great and small we witness a voluntary surrender of something beneficial to oneself (with one's own life as the exemplar and upper limit) for another's sake. The fact that we tend to admire and revere those who act sacrificially suggests that sacrifice is a type of human excellence.

My suggestion is that whatever it is that inclines us to make sacrifices on behalf of others is that original goodness of which a desire for self-harm is a corruption. We have a capacity to do something that is, in some real though perhaps not ultimate sense, harmful to us. At its best, this capacity is used for the good of others. Maybe even for our own good, as when we undergo suffering that is for our own benefit, like the weight lifting that tears our muscles only to make them stronger. Plausibly then, this same capacity can be corrupted, when by it we do what is bad for others or for ourselves.

Thinking of self-harm as a corruption of the human capacity for sacrifice makes the phenomenon less anomalous, though of course not fully explicable. It also raises a new question, about the mystery of our capacity for sacrifice.

But here, I have a sense that we are probing something deep and good at the heart of being, a pattern or direction of things suggesting that we're at our most human when we're most humane. The rigors of parenting, the patience of teaching, the Christian martyrs and their crucified God, all attest to this paradoxical possibility that we are at our best when we willingly forsake what is good for us and offer it to someone else. If we are on the right track, then not only do humans seek the good even in cases of suicide and self-harm, but that very capacity for self-harm is but a corruption of a capacity that is ordered to the good. "Unless a grain of wheat falls into the earth and dies, it remains alone; but if it dies, it bears much fruit."[8]

HAPPINESS

But what, after all, is the good? Or at least, what is the good for us? It can't be sacrifice all the way down; otherwise, sacrifice has no point. At the same time, whatever the good is, it must be within our power to achieve it through sacrifice; otherwise, sacrificial acts are not as good as we make them out to be. Boethius was unequivocal: the good that we seek, in everything we do, from our noblest actions to our wickedest, is happiness. "The whole concern of men, which the effort of a multitude of pursuits keeps

8. John 12:24.

busy, moves by different roads, yet strives to arrive at one and the same end, that of happiness" (C 3.2p, Tester, 233).

Given Boethius's own experience standing before the Roman senate to defend Albinus against the charge of treason, a defense which he probably anticipated would get him into trouble, his claim that the good we always seek is happiness should sound more than a little puzzling.

To solve the puzzle, we must attend closely to an important distinction Lady Philosophy makes. Not all translators are sensitive to the fact that she has two words that are acceptably translated as "happiness" but actually signify distinct concepts in *Consolation*. The terms are *felicitas* and *beatitudo*, from which we get our words "felicity" and "beatitude"—sometimes used as synonyms for "happiness." To begin to grasp the distinction between these terms, consider the difference between a happy mood and a deep sense of well-being.

Felicity is the happiness of a happy mood that comes and goes, and often is not in our control. A good night's sleep and the perfect cup of coffee might have you starting the day pretty happy, but then bad traffic on your commute has you clenching your teeth by the time you get to the office. You might be feeling a little down or stressed at the end of the day, but then a good run or a well-made Manhattan lifts your spirits. Felicity is the sort of thing subject to these contingent and ephemeral moments. Unless you are a Stoic master, these ups and downs are an unavoidable part of life. And even the Stoic master will concede that of all these "indifferent" things from which we should practice detachment, some are more welcome than others.

Beatitude, by contrast, is the happiness of well-being. As an ideal, it is perfect joy, the sort of joy available only to someone completely virtuous enjoying perfect health and harmonious relationships in an environment one hundred percent auspicious for acting and thinking with excellence. None of us has beatitude in that ideal sense. But we approximate beatitude when we are, in the way feasible for us here and now, "firing on all cylinders": thinking and acting virtuously in all areas of life. Beatitude does not come and go like felicity. It is a deeply rooted way of life, bringing with it a felt sense of one's whole life as a great and welcome good.

A life subject to felicity, but without beatitude, is knocked around by the circumstances of life. You might say that the merely felicitous person is at nature's whim, made to conform to external circumstances, now high, now low, now middling. But the life of beatitude radiates outward, confronting the circumstances of life with joyful boldness and conforming them to its own tranquil beauty.

But it must be said that here and now, subject as we are to fortune and ultimately death, the sort of beatitude we can reasonably hope for falls well short of perfection. It would be no mark of virtue, for example, for someone not to be deeply grieved by the death of a loved one or to be indifferent to the suffering of others. Recall that for Boethius, right ethical conduct consists mostly in apprehending the goodness of things and responding to that goodness in appropriate, commensurate ways. This holds for small goods no less than great goods like people. I take it as a sign I am not wholly reprobate that when I squash non-stinging, non-biting bugs in my house, I feel a little bad about it. By the same measure, it is a sign of my friend's virtue that he will do all he can not to kill bugs on purpose. And everyone hopes that at least one person will one day look on them as lovingly as my eldest son looks on a single fuzzy caterpillar.

Correct response to goodness often takes the form of delight—the heart-melting, cozy delight in a baby's smile or the wondrous delight in a hawk's flight. But by the same sensitivity to goodness, the upright soul is also sorrowful or compassionate or angry in response to good things harmed or threatened, not

69

only because they might happen to belong to us, but because they are good.

The readiness to protect, even unto violence, can also be an appropriate response to good things threatened. Anger, rage, even hatred have their place in the good life, when the good life confronts wickedness. Faramir, second son of the Steward of Gondor, wise and noble prince, is brave as they come. But he does not fight for the fun of it. "War must be," he explains, "while we defend our lives against a destroyer who would devour all; but I do not love the bright sword for its sharpness, nor the arrow for its swiftness, nor the warrior for his glory. I love only that which they defend."[9]

Sorrow, too (too often!), is the good way to respond to goods lost or harmed. The death of one's spouse or friend grieves more than another's because we know best those closest to us and therefore see better what a loss that person is not just to oneself but, in some mysterious sense, to the world. Even Jesus weeps at the death of his friend Lazarus.[10] This allowance for negative emotions in the happy life is one of the practical advantages of Boethius over his Stoic friends. Marcus Aurelius echoed his tradition when he wrote that "to turn against anything that comes to pass is a separation from Nature."[11] On this view, untroubled acceptance, even of bereavement, is the only acceptable response to anything that happens to us. But this isn't right. Grief and other forms of sadness, not to mention anger, are natural and good ways to respond to some of the harms and losses to which our nature makes us vulnerable.

Beatitude, then, in the nonideal form that is the only form we can find it here and now, enfolds within itself the full range of human emotions, even moods. But the one who has beatitude feels in accordance with correct apprehension of goodness. And

9. Tolkien, *Lord of the Rings* 4.5, 672.
10. See John 11:35.
11. Marcus Aurelius, *Meditations* 2.16, trans. Farquharson, 14.

the one who has beatitude never despairs, or never wallows in despair, if he from time to time stumbles into the slough of despond.

This focus on the emotional life accompanying beatitude is necessary for showing the sharp contrast between beatitude and felicity. Felicity, as I said, is like a happy mood; it is therefore incompatible with emotions like sorrow or anger. But the root of beatitude is not a mood. It is a form of life from which a complex bouquet of emotions flower, each in its proper season. But in all seasons, the one who enjoys beatitude is attuned to goodness, without and within, dwells and is united with goodness, and is therefore constantly nourished by goodness.

Lady Philosophy, having disabused Boethius of the false idea that goods of fortune could give him what he truly seeks, now prepares to show him the way to beatitude. When she said that "the whole concern of men . . . strives to arrive at one and the same end, that of happiness," the word she used for "happiness" is *beatitudo* (C 3.2p, Tester, 233). Goods of fortune, she says, can at best only bring *felicitas*, but the *beatitudo* she wishes on Boethius is the "true felicity" (*veram felicitatem*), the reality of which mere *felicitas* is only a shadow (C 3.1p).

In what follows, I will revert to the more familiar word, "happiness." But it must be kept in mind that from here on out, unless otherwise specified, the sort of happiness under discussion is beatitude, not felicity.

EXPERIENCE MACHINE

I have described the emotions accompanying happiness (remember: beatitude) as the flowers and not the root of happiness. This root is something well described as well-being. Thomas Aquinas is the philosopher most closely associated with the idea that being or existence itself is a kind of activity. Activities are the sorts of things that can be done well or poorly. So, well-being is doing a good job at the activity of existing. For things like us, then, whose existence takes the form of human life, well-being is the total activity of human living done well. Doing a good job at being human: that is happiness.

Aristotle is probably the first philosopher to describe the happiness we all aim at as a kind of total life activity: "The human good turns out to be the activity of soul in conformity with excellence."[12] We will examine Boethius's own take on the activity of the happy life and some of the conditions necessary for sustaining that activity in chapters 5 and 6. But for now, we need to consider an important challenge to the idea of happiness as a kind of life activity.

I am haunted by a thought experiment first put forward by the philosopher Robert Nozick (1938–2002), a thought experiment usually named after its central concept, the Experience Machine. Here it is in Nozick's own words: "Suppose there were an experience machine that would give you any experience that you desired. Superduper neuropsychologists could stimulate your brain so that you would think and feel you were writing a great novel, or making a friend, or reading an interesting book. All the time you would be floating in a tank, with electrodes attached to your brain. Should you plug into this machine for life, pre-programming your life's experiences? . . . Of course, while in the tank you won't know that you're there; you'll think it's all actually happening. . . . Would you plug in?"[13]

Nozick presupposes none of us would plug in. He does not even argue that we should not plug in. Instead, he offers three reasons he presumes everyone would have for not plugging in. "First," he says, "we want to *do* certain things, and not just have the experience of doing them." Second, "we want to *be* a certain way, to be a certain sort of person." And third, "an experience

12. Aristotle, *Nicomachean Ethics* 1.7 1098a.
13. Nozick, *Anarchy, State, and Utopia*, 42–43.

machine limits us to a man-made reality, to a world no deeper or more important than that which people can construct. There is no *actual* contact with any deeper reality, though the experience of it can be simulated."[14]

In the Experience Machine you don't do anything; you're just a passive subject of experience, "floating in a tank," "an indeterminate blob." Nor do you have a determinate character: the Machine might give you the experience of doing heroic deeds, but you aren't thereby brave. In the Machine you might win the annual prize for World's Best Husband, but you won't actually be loving or faithful, or even married.

And in the Experience Machine, there is nothing beyond what another philosopher has called "the immanent frame."[15] The Machine can simulate the experience of exploring unknown worlds, or making discoveries, or composing a symphony, or mystical union with God. But your actual contact with reality is limited to the Machine and what its technicians can program it to simulate based on what is already known and has already been experienced.

Nozick asked rhetorically, trying to imagine someone having a little attraction to the Machine, "*What else can matter to us, other than how our lives feel from the inside?*" His answer, of course (and mine too, and Aristotle's and Boethius's and so on), is this: plenty! That's the whole point of the thought experiment! By considering how unattractive the Experience Machine is, we come to see in a startlingly clear way just how much it means to us to be doing things, and to have a certain character, and to be in touch with what is really real. Pleasant experiences are good but are not worth having at the expense of the real activity of living.

It is a common experience of teachers, as we age, to find it ever more difficult to understand our students, the further

14. Nozick, *Anarchy, State, and Utopia*, 43.
15. Taylor, *A Secular Age*, 542.

removed we are from them in time, and the further removed we are from ourselves when we were their age. Recently, I have felt this especially keenly, as so many of my students in this decade say they would, eagerly, plug into an Experience Machine if the technicians ever invent one.

Every year, I lead a discussion with my students on the Experience Machine. I don't tell them right away what Nozick or I think about it. I describe the experience of being in the Machine as attractively as possible. Once we're all clear on the details, I ask for a show of hands: Who would plug in? When I started doing this, about fifteen years ago, I would typically get one or two hands raised. Most recently (in the fall of 2023), about half raised their hands. And this wasn't an anomaly: the number of raised hands has been trending up for a few years now.

I blame the iPhone. Others may blame climate change, geopolitical unrest, or Donald Trump. But they must remember that in 1974, the year Nozick published the book introducing the Experience Machine, students would have been dealing with comparably worrisome issues: the Cold War, Vietnam, Richard Nixon, overpopulation,[16] environmental catastrophe,[17] and polyester suits. I was not around to poll students back then, but it is telling that Nozick does not argue for, but presupposes agreement about, rejecting the Machine.

What the 1970s did not have is the iPhone, or even the internet or the personal computer. A lot of people complain these days about the way in which various activities on the internet have become compulsive. The phenomenon of "binge-watching" is like this too—not to mention bingeing in general. iPhones and other smartphones and tablets make it easier to indulge the compulsions, since most of us carry them around with us all the time. Many of us recognize that life shouldn't be like this. But we

16. Ehrlich, *The Population Bomb*.
17. Carson, *Silent Spring*.

struggle to amend. Part of cultivating detachment is recognizing these goods for what they really are: tools of communication and information storage, not devices for immersion in a virtual world.[18] But without great effort and a little countercultural flare, the default for modern people is to be functionally plugged in, through their phones or other screens, to a sort of meager prototype of a fully developed Experience Machine. If we have already adopted the beta version, why wouldn't we jump on board when the final is generally available?

To be fair, many students are persuadable about whether they'd plug in. What seems to hit home for them, once pointed out, is the fact that while the Machine can simulate the experience of having deep personal relationships, you do not in fact have that sort of relationship with anyone while plugged in. The longing for relationship keeps them tethered to the real.

The desire for simulated reality, it seems to me, is one of those ways humans can go astray in their pursuit of happiness. They desire happiness—the real thing—but make the mistake of thinking they can get that through simulated means, means that sometimes are pleasanter and easier than the real work of living, it must be said. The only argument for those tempted in this direction—other than lots of cheerleading for the real, of the sort I do in my classes—is to point out that the simulation could not entice as it does if we did not have a prior orientation to the real thing.

MYSTERIOUS IGNORANCE

In Bruce Marshall's little-read but widely quoted 1945 novel *The World, The Flesh, and Father Smith*—a novel I have not read—the titular priest, Father Smith, explains to a woman who thinks religion is a substitute for sex, that "the young man who rings the

18. Crouch, *The Life We're Looking For*, 135–38.

bell at the brothel is unconsciously looking for God."[19] If I am right about the Experience Machine, whether or not the young man is looking for God, he is at least looking for a wife. Fornication, after all, is a simulation of marriage that decouples copulation from the mutual lifelong commitment that the emotional attachment and procreative potential of sex disposes us to pursue.

The young man at the brothel and the Experience Machine (including its smartphone beta version) are examples of a pervasive type of human activity that is an enigma. We seek the shadow instead of the reality, the image rather than the exemplar. And our current examples notwithstanding, this type of activity is not pervasively bad. Contact sports are simulated violence, civilized by elaborate rules. Some video games simulate valorous deeds and intrepid discovery. A great deal of storytelling immerses us in fictional worlds with fictional characters through whom we can vicariously inhabit those worlds and their conflicts. Physical training simulates physical effort for real-life tasks and is often undertaken to improve our ability to do real-life tasks.

Sometimes, we are confused about what is the shadow and what the reality. A hermeneutic of suspicion encourages us to view our noblest, most wholesome, most civilized ideals and practices as the shadows of a more brutish or merely biological reality. Nietzsche wants us to treat the great Christian ideal of the love of neighbor as an ingenious ruse by the weak to gain power over the strong.[20] Marx (1818–1883) believes all of art, the family, and religion are tools of class oppression.[21] Freud thinks that ideals about romantic love and marriage are highly complex cultural constructions developed to help us balance the shame of, and overwhelming desire for, sex.[22] Michel Foucault (1926–1984), learning from these and other "masters of suspicion,"

19. Stanton, "FactChecker: C.S. Lewis and G.K. Chesterton Quotes."
20. Nietzsche, *On the Genealogy of Morals* 1.
21. Marx and Engels, *Communist Manifesto* 2.
22. Freud, *Civilization and its Discontents* 4.

thinks there is no end to shadows: social life is power struggle all the way down.[23] *Abusus tollit usum*, after all. What these all have in common is the conviction that human life boils down to something baser and uglier than most of us are willing to think it is: mere urges for sex and violence in the service of survival. All our righteousness is filthy rags, indeed![24]

If the masters of suspicion think civilization and morality and religion are the shadows of which sex and power are the realities, earlier thinkers hold exactly the reverse. Plato thought our erotic desires were meant to unite us with the Form of the Beautiful itself and are bound to be frustrated if we linger in the shadow of mere sensual satisfaction.[25] Thomas Aquinas taught that the purpose of political authority was not the personal benefit of the sovereign but of the people over whom he reigns.[26] Dante united these erotic and political themes in his *Paradiso*, offering the sublimest poetic vision ever achieved of the classical ideal of the sovereign *summum bonum* whose goodness summons every creature to glory not only or even primarily through legislation but rather attraction.[27] Bonaventure (1217–1274) and thinkers under his influence, like Robert Bellarmine (1542–1621), descried in every art, science, or craft a peculiar path to God.[28] In every leper, Francis of Assisi (1181–1226) found the face of the Christ he adored. Samuel Taylor Coleridge (1772–1834), after long struggle, saw every creature as a representation of the mind of God.[29] In the bleak midwinter, G.K. Chesterton (1874–1936) thought that when we gather by the hearth and warm ourselves by a merry fire when all outside is sleet and snow, we can start to see "That the

23. Foucault, *History of Sexuality* 1.4.2.

24. See Isaiah 64:6.

25. Plato, *Symposium* 204d–212a.

26. Aquinas, *De regno* 2.

27. Dante, *Paradise* 1.103–42, 26.4–67.

28. Bonaventure, *Itinerarium mentis in Deum*, in *Works of St. Bonaventure*; Bellarmine, *Ascent of the Mind to God*.

29. Coleridge, *Biographia Literaria*, in Collected Works 7/1: 304–5.

midst of the earth is a raging mirth / And the heart of the earth a star."[30] What all these thinkers have in common is the conviction not only that the ordinary human institutions of the family, the state, the liberal arts, the church, and the pub are wholesome and healthy for our merely natural lives, but also that these somehow point to something beyond themselves, some transcendent and better reality that keeps us hopeful and energetic in the midst of so much frustration, wickedness, ruin, and decay.

It is hard to judge between the masters of suspicion who tell us the noblest things are the shadows and the basest the realities, and the old masters who tell us the basest are shadows of the noblest. Can we judge?

Here is a thought that has helped me: It is good to be suspicious of the masters of suspicion. As C.S. Lewis observed nearly a hundred years ago, it is only reasonable to decide that the more beautiful or noble is a shadow of the ugly or base if you have already granted that the fundamental nature of reality is more likely to be ugly or base than beautiful or noble.[31] But the grounds for that judgment are at best just as good as the grounds for the opposite judgment, that reality is fundamentally beautiful or noble.

Here is another helpful thought, also from Lewis: You might think the masters of suspicion have more the whiff of the real on the grounds that their philosophy runs against so much wishful thinking about how we'd like the world to be. It smacks of showing up illusions and brutal honesty. But the charge of wishful thinking cuts both ways:[32] Why can't the crusty old traditionalist about religion and morality simply accuse the Marxist or Nietzschean or Freudian of wishful thinking when they reduce everything to economics and power and sex? Isn't that just how they want the world to be? In short, the wishful thinking charge

30. Chesterton, "The Feast of Snow," in *Collected Works*, 10:68.
31. Lewis, *Pilgrim's Regress*, 59.
32. Lewis, *Pilgrim's Regress*, 63–64.

does not in the least stack the deck in favor of the masters of suspicion.

And a third: In general, you'd expect that a shadow or a copy would feel somehow less *detailed* than the original. You'd expect it to lack some of the qualities of the original, preserving enough for it to be a reminder of the original but not enough to stand in for the real thing. If this is right, then we'd have a predictive rule of thumb: where there are two things and one is the copy of the other, the less detailed, less vivid, is likely to be the copy. But then we'd expect things like marriage and kingship and art to be more real, and more of what we really want, than sex and power and economic security.

These three helpful thoughts don't on their own decide anything. But they tilt in favor of those old masters who have held that ordinary things are shadows of higher things, not lower things. This keeps the door open for a transcendent answer to the questions about what is the shadow and what the reality.

Entertain, for now, the possibility that as a general rule, the lower is the shadow of the higher, rather than the other way around: that the young husband on his wedding day is more like the mystic seeking God than the lecher seeking a prostitute. Then, where Foucault assumes the shadows go all the way down, we might start to wonder, how high do they go? Are there shadows of shadows, up and up, and if so, how high? We will consider Boethius's answer to this question over the next two chapters.

Consider how little we have said so far about what happiness really is. It is not to be found in goods of fortune. It is the sort of thing we pursue always, whether we act well or badly—even in self-harm, even in simulation. It is not a good mood but total activity of human living done well. It is the sort of thing we might pursue imperfectly under shadows or images rather than directly.

Yes, but *what is it*? Well, that is a very good question. For an answer, let us return to Lady Philosophy. So far her therapeutic efforts have been aimed at detaching Boethius from the false hopes of the goods of fortune. From here on out, her aim is to reorient Boethius's longing to hope for a true happiness that can be sought even by a prisoner on death row.

5

Ideal Happiness

Back when Lady Philosophy used the gentle medicine of rhetoric to hasten Boethius's cure, she had said that Lady Fortune, through the sorts of goods she can bestow and withdraw, "is not responsible for anything of beauty that you have ever had or lost" (C 2.1p, 31). Fortune's goods offer only "counterfeit happiness" (*falsa felicitas*) (C 2.1p, 32). Later on, Lady Philosophy's medicine becomes more bitter to the taste but sweeter and more satisfying once digested (C 3.1p). She reaffirms that the goods of fortune cannot make a man happy but now suggests these goods are not as alien to true happiness as she first made them out to be.

On the one hand, she says, each of these goods of fortune is a false appearance of happiness (*beatitudinis species falsa*). But on the other hand, in the very same paragraph, she says that each is a faint image (*imago tenuis*) of that true good we all seek (C 3.3p), and just a few pages later says more emphatically that these are imperfect goods (*inperfecta bona*) and images of the true good (*imagines veri boni*) (C 3.9p).

There is the threat of contradiction here, a threat neutralized by reflecting on the proper function of images. Imagine a soldier deployed to a distant land who carries around with him a picture of a woman. "Here's my special lady friend," he says to a comrade, showing him the picture. "Hey, lucky man. I bet you miss her." Now try to imagine just how odd it would be if our soldier replied, "Miss her? What do you mean, she's right here! I just showed her to you!"

This creepy conversation underscores an important point about pictures of people: pictures of people aren't people. People who think they are, like our poor soldier, are deluded. But there is nothing delusional about the use of pictures as images of people. Suppose his response to the statement "I bet you miss her" had been, "Yeah. I got three more months here. Then we're getting married. Gonna go on a honeymoon to Hawaii. Can't wait." In this case the picture has done its job: called before both their minds the real person whose picture it is.

The goods of fortune, at their best, are like pictures of happiness. Lady Philosophy emphatically wants Boethius to understand that it is as delusional to mistake any of them for happiness as it is for our soldier to mistake the picture for his fiancée. But that doesn't mean the goods of fortune are worthless, any more than it means the picture is worthless.

For each type of good that men mistakenly pursue as their ultimate good, Lady Philosophy wants Boethius to understand not only, negatively, that it cannot produce happiness, but also, constructively, what it is about that type of good that makes it apt to be mistaken for the ultimate good. Ultimately, each of the good things we pursue does have some genuine likeness to the true happiness we seek. Pursued accordingly, they are like "images of the true good"; pursued as though they were the ultimate good, they offer only "counterfeit happiness."

So, it is now time to say what's so good about the good things we commonly pursue. No, money cannot make us truly happy. But it's still pretty good. Those with money can get many of the things they need and want far more efficiently than by their own labor. Think about it like this: You need food, shelter, and clothing. You don't know how to provide yourself with all these things by your own labor, except maybe in a very basic way. But even if you could, your limited time and energy would be almost totally absorbed by these labors. In some mysterious way, money dramatically increases the productive power of your labor. You devote a lot of time to your job doing one thing, fixing cars, let's say, or healing bodies. By devoting so much time to one thing, you get rather good at it. In exchange, you get money, with which you can acquire the fruits of other specialists' labors. On your own, you'd provide for your own needs crudely and inefficiently; in a money economy, we get a community of specialists providing higher-quality goods for each other at a fraction of the cost of time and energy.

Put like this, it's no wonder that we long for money. And Lady Philosophy concedes the reasonableness of this longing. But she observes that we don't desire money for its own sake but rather for what it can get us. It has merely *instrumental* value and therefore does not have the nature of an *ultimate* good. But what it is good for is genuinely good: the satisfaction of many of our needs and wants. It stands to reason that those with a lot of money, at least with respect to the things that money can buy, are more *self-sufficient* than those with less. When we desire money, Lady Philosophy says, we're really desiring the sufficiency money offers (C 3.3p).

Sufficiency is a good thing to want! The problem, of course, is that money can't make us fully sufficient. We will eventually die. And, as Lady Philosophy observes, those with money are at constant risk of losing it and in constant anxiety about that risk.

So here's the good part about money: having it really does increase our ability to provide for ourselves and our loved ones. Sufficiency is good, and so it is good to want it, and so it is rational to want the money that grants it. But here's the bad part about money: it can't fully guarantee sufficiency both because it is the sort of thing that can be lost and because there are things we need and want that money cannot buy.

Lady Philosophy makes similar points about other types of goods that we humans tend to seek mistakenly as ultimate goods. For each type, she states what it is that makes that mistaken pursuit make sense. We long to be honorable (*dignissimum veneratione*) and therefore seek public honors and a good reputation. We long for power (*summa potentia*) and therefore seek positions of influence or alliance with those who have them. We long for fame (*claritas*) and therefore pursue publicity through noteworthy deeds. We long for bliss (*gaudium et laetitium*) and therefore pursue sensual pleasures (C 3.2p).

So here are five types of goods we humans often pursue as though they are the highest goods: sufficiency, honorableness, power, fame, bliss. And the commonly pursued means by which we aim to achieve these goods are, respectively, money, honors, positions of influence, publicity, and sensual pleasures.

Each of the means by which each type of good is commonly pursued is ultimately defective: at their best, they can only offer a taste of what is truly sought, a shadow or image of the total reality. To pursue any of these means as though it could provide the real thing is to be as deluded as the soldier treating his photograph like it was his fiancée. But it would be almost as deluded to discard the picture altogether on the grounds that it was not the fiancée. There is a place for the picture and a place for the fiancée: use of the one keeps us mindful of and eager for the other. The good things of the world—money, honors, positions of influence, publicity, sensual pleasures—at their best, confer something like a photograph of true happiness. The goal is to acknowledge what is good in them but settle for nothing less than the real thing.

THE DEFINITION OF HAPPINESS

Out of the five snapshots of happiness just considered—sufficiency, honor, influence, fame, pleasure—Lady Philosophy brings before our minds a unified vision of true happiness. These five *together*, considered in their most ideal extreme, compose the definition of ideal happiness. The startling claim is that at their upper limit, these five converge as *one and the same thing*, happiness.

Before considering Lady Philosophy's reasoning for that claim, however, we need to do just a bit of work to stay sympathetic with our man Boethius. His priorities and occupations, we might well think, are not very much like our own. He was a wealthy Roman senator and ambitious scholar who enjoyed the limelight and continued to seek political preferment until his downfall. Many of us—myself included, I must admit—might not at first find much sympathy with Lady Philosophy's definition of happiness. I say, *at first*, however, because I think she is right, or near enough right as makes no difference.

Sufficiency. This might connote a sort of rugged individualism that many would find unattractive. Isn't part of our good as human beings our shared life together, and aren't our mutual dependencies at least the glue if not the substance of this shared life? The answer is yes. If I am hungry or thirsty or sick, it is good of you to help me. Help is the form charity takes where one has deprivation and the other abundance. But wouldn't it be better if both of us had food and drink and good health? Life together would be much more enjoyable (all else being equal). And supposing we never had to die? We could just go on enjoying life together. Think of the ideal of sufficiency, then, not so much as independence or individualism but more like *wholeness*—there's nothing about either your embodied life or your character that holds you back from full participation in the good for human beings, including, of course, its social goods. It's in the sense of wholeness, rather than independence, that Paul tells us (in

Jerome's Latin translation of the Bible) that God can give us all that we need for sufficiency—clearly Paul understands sufficiency in a way that is compatible with dependence (on God).[1]

Honor, Influence, Fame. Most of us do not win Most Valuable Player awards, or Academy Awards, or Nobel Prizes. Most of us do not run for political office or even want to. Most of us would find fame, in the ordinary sense of being a celebrity, intolerable. So the honor-seeking, influence-seeking, fame-seeking lives can therefore seem not only quite rarefied, out of touch with ordinary people like us, but also unattractive. And yet, desires for these types of goods manifest both in extraordinary and ordinary ways. You may have no desire to be a senator, but you might harbor an ambition to be not just a fireman but a fire chief, not just a lawyer but a partner, not just a framer but a foreman. But even if you don't, you are acting on your desire for influence literally every time you so much as ask the person dining next to you to please pass the salt. Perhaps you have expressed no interest in being a contestant on *The Great British Baking Show*, but you will be disappointed if your pie is not the family favorite at next year's Thanksgiving dinner. You might scoff at *Time* magazine's Person of the Year issue, yet long to hear your parents say, "I'm really proud of you," or your husband say, "You're an amazing woman."

Let us grant that movie stars in Hollywood and politicians in Washington are, as a rule, obsessive and excessive in their pursuit of honors, influence, and fame. But their excess suggests a golden mean. After all, there can be a deficiency with respect to these things: the sometimes annoying, often heartbreaking comportment of those who are extremely self-effacing, timid, deferential, or slovenly. Perhaps it is better to err on the side of thinking too little of oneself than too much, but both are unbecoming. We want to be admired by others, we want our achievements known and acknowledged, we want to be in communities that practice

---

1. See 2 Corinthians 9:8; Asbell, "The Philosophical Background of *Sufficientia*," 4.

an easy give-and-take, each making reasonable demands on the others and ready to reciprocate in turn—not in a transactional way but in an "I'm here for you, man" sort of way. All of this is to say that ideal happiness is inescapably social.

Pleasure. Does pleasure need a defense? There may be certain ascetic and exceptionally high-minded souls out there who would think it beneath the dignity of what is noblest in us for pleasure to have a place in the perfectly happy life. But most of us aren't them. Sure, we may be in need of a lot of training about what we find most pleasurable. We may have disordered desires for pleasure taken in the wrong things or the wrong ways or at the wrong times. But few of us would question the goodness of pleasure as such.

Still, the category of pleasure is more complex than merely sensual pleasure at first suggests. It's helpful to distinguish those pleasures that are essentially sensory from those that are not. The sensory pleasures are, paradigmatically, the pleasures of food, drink, and sex. But they are far more wide-ranging than this canonical trio suggests. Consider your favorite smells, or beautiful landscapes or works of art that delight the eyes, or the sound of music, or the feeling of a back scratch or stepping into a hot bath. To be sure, there often is something more than sensory going on in the experience of these pleasures—obviously so, in the case of music or landscapes or artworks—but it remains that these are pleasures we can only have by means of the senses.

But here's another kind of pleasure: the sense of satisfaction in a job well done or a deep sense of contentment with how one's life is going. It seems clear to me that these are pleasures; it is indisputable that they are pleasant. If pleasure is part of the perfectly happy life, plausibly what this means is, minimally, that the one who is enjoying a perfectly happy life has just this sort of reflective pleasure: the enjoyment of well-being is part of what it is to have well-being. Yes, here and now, well-being often requires or invites the experience of suffering, a suffering that might make it difficult or impossible for the sufferer to have that subjective enjoyment of well-being, however admirable his or her life. But here we are talking about idealized happiness: If human life were perfect, would pleasure have a place in that perfection? Of course it would.

So Lady Philosophy and Boethius get it right when they include sufficiency, honor, influence, fame, and pleasure as five components of happiness. And they've left nothing out that can't plausibly be thought of as a subcategory of one of these five.

Now here is the interesting part: Lady Philosophy argues that these five are one and the same thing. "This thing"—happiness—"that is by nature one and the same has been divided by human perversity" (C 3.9p, 83). To show the unity of happiness, Lady Philosophy reasons with Boethius to show that of these five parts of happiness, it is impossible to have one—fully, ideally—without having all the others.

Take *sufficiency*. It clearly implies *power*. We lack power precisely to the extent we are laid low by illness, injury, or vice. But the one with sufficiency and power truly is most *honorable*, genuinely worthy of honor and not merely successful at winning awards. A person of such excellence would not fail to become *famous*, since power and sufficiency logically guarantee success in excellent action for oneself and others. Finally, such a person could not fail to find life perfectly *delightful*, at least in that reflective sense of awareness of and delight in one's own well-being (C 3.9p).

This series of entailments reinforces the argument Lady Philosophy has been pursuing all along: no one can find happiness through any of the routes people commonly pursue—wealth, honors, positions of influence, publicity, sensual pleasures. The real reason, it turns out, is that each of these at best pursues not just a *shadow* of true happiness but the *shadow of an aspect* of true happiness, an aspect that cannot be achieved except by achieving all aspects together.

So Boethius has finally discovered the nature of true happiness! It is the state of the person who is "perfectly sufficient, powerful, renowned, and joyful" (C 3.9p, 84). He has unlocked the secret, found the low door in the wall, the well at the world's end, the fountain of youth! All that remains is to reach out and take it!

But this is obviously absurd. At best, this is an ideal. But it is an impossible ideal. And a thousand Stoic sages rise up in scoffing protest that this is not an ideal fit for mortal man, doomed to die.

But Boethius is not naive. Lady Philosophy asks, "Do you think there is anything in these mortal, transitory affairs that can bring about such a condition?" And the prisoner replies, "Not at all, I think. You have demonstrated this well enough and no further arguments are needed" (C 3.9p, 85).

Having conceded the impossibility of happiness, what more is there to say? Isn't a hope for the impossible just the sort of hope Lady Philosophy told Boethius to abandon at the beginning of therapy? Well, yes. But impossible is a strong word.

ON THE IMPOSSIBLE

The pursuit of ideal happiness might seem quixotic at best, tragic at worst. We'll consider the tragedy soon, but for now let's think about Don Quixote. It would be totally sensible to tilt at windmills if the windmills were really giants, as Don Quixote believed them to be. But as they are windmills, tilting at them is not good policy. But if there really are giants, and all you have is a horse and a lance, it would be insensible not to tilt. Only in the absence of giants is the knight ridiculous.

Those of us who continue—as grown-ups, into middle age, with at least a fair share of hard knocks—to long without cynicism or irony for unalloyed beatitude may well seem even more ridiculous than the knight. For the giants, if they are unreal, are at least possible; whereas the sort of happiness Lady Philosophy defines appears to be not only unreal but impossible. The conditions of human life as we know it, and for that matter the second law of thermodynamics, do not permit the sempiternal sufficiency required for ideal happiness. Life as we know it means that however good life gets, however virtuous we are, we are all going to die, and we know it. Even in seasons of good health, the fact of our deaths is ambient, like cicadas in summer.

Thus, it would seem safe to conclude that Lady Philosophy's definition of happiness expresses something impossible. If the definition of a squircle is "square circle," we know there are no squircles because we know squircles, so defined, to be impossible. Likewise, if the definition of a truly happy man is one who is totally sufficient, powerful, renowned, honorable, and joyful, then we know there are no truly happy men because there cannot be a mere mortal who possesses all these qualities.

Jesus Christ is reported to have said that it is easier for a camel to go through the eye of a needle than for a rich man to enter heaven.[2] But he added, perhaps with a wink, that with God all things are possible.[3] Reflecting on this Bible story, C. S. Lewis wrote: "All things (e.g. a camel's journey through / A needle's eye) are possible, it's true. / But picture how the camel feels, squeezed out / In one long bloody thread, from tail to snout."[4]

What Jesus implies is that it is not in fact impossible either for a camel to go through the eye of a needle or for a rich man to enter heaven. But neither statement shouts its possibility, so to speak, or provides an instruction manual. To grasp their possibility requires a special effort of the imagination, such as Lewis's. It is like this also with true happiness. It is possible. It is not obvious

2. See Matthew 19:23–24.
3. See Matthew 19:26.
4. Lewis, "Epigrams and Epitaphs," in *Poems.*

how it is possible. But the failure to grasp possibility does not imply successfully grasping impossibility.

If you could get yourself to believe that it is possible to be truly happy, you might be able to hope for true happiness. Notice that if you incorrectly believe that a possible thing is impossible, you can't really be said to hope for the thing you think is impossible. And if you believe incorrectly that an impossible thing is possible, you can go on wanting it as long as you believe it to be possible. So, too, if you believe correctly that an impossible thing is impossible, you can't really hope for it. It's just a fact about what hope is: it's a firm desire for a good that is *difficult* to achieve or *unlikely* to come about, but not for a good that is really and truly *impossible*.

There is a famous painting by George Frederic Watts (1817–1904), all in muted coppers and blues. A slender woman sits on a bare sphere, her neck and shoulders drooped, eyes blindfolded, hands clutching a harp. All of the strings of the harp are broken but one. The painting is called *Hope*.

Here, I want to do no more than preserve a single string of the harp of happiness. Later, we will follow Boethius on a more ambitious quest. But all we need at this stage is to secure the bare possibility of true happiness. To do this, we invoke both reason and imagination.

Try to imagine the conditions of human life adequately changed for a man to be the proper subject of happiness while remaining still a man. If we imagine some series of psychological and physiological changes to human nature so radical that the result cannot in any valid sense still be called human, then however happy we imagine that new thing to be, we are not imagining human happiness. Yet, if we imagine human nature too close to what it already is, rationality will continue to protest that such a giddy thing as man cannot be truly happy. The religious concepts of *heaven* and *eternal life* give us what we need at this point—remember, this is simply about establishing bare possibility, not committing to a religious way of life. The hope of those who believe in heaven is that we will be there, but everything that keeps us from perfect happiness in this life will be taken away: no sickness, no death, no disordered desiring; in these conditions, we are free to go on being happy forever.

If talk of the afterlife is distracting due to its association with religion, we can turn instead to the contemporary anti-aging and transhumanist movements. No one active in these movements believes that we will be able to prevent death any time soon, but their logic is that there is no acceptable natural limit to human life. If technology and medicine eventually enable every human being to live to a hundred and twenty with the body of a forty-year-old and then die without pain, that will be quite an accomplishment. But within the logic of the movement, that will be just a beginning. They will not be done until all our bodies have been converted to bionic diamonds and death comes to no one except those who choose it.

We cannot take for granted that the prolongation of life they will have to offer is a prolongation of a life we can call our own. But that concern is better developed elsewhere. For now, remember, we're simply considering the bare possibility of the sort of happiness Lady Philosophy defines. And insofar as biological need, finite resources, injury, illness, and death prevent us from achieving that sort of happiness, to go on believing it is possible to be happy we must envision human nature suitably enhanced, either in heaven or in the lab. However unlikely these religious and technological dreams might seem, they check out at the level of mere possibility. And that is all we need them to do right now.

TRAGEDY

But some have thought that even if we could by God or science get out from under the stone of Tantalus,[5] we humans still could not be perfectly happy. The most famous of these is Bernard Williams (1929–2003), who argued influentially but sloppily that an immortal life would inevitably become boring and so undesirable.[6] If your immortality depended on regularly taking a special elixir, he imagined, eventually you would desire to stop taking it and you would be rational to do so.

My mom is an expert quilter. She's always working on a quilt. She is not as good a quilter as can be; she has other interests to occupy her time and maybe the world's best quilters have some special talent that she does not possess, so that no matter how many hours a day she spent quilting she'd never enter that elite class. I have no opinion about this. I just know that my mom makes very good and beautiful quilts, and that she enjoys making them. I have not asked her, and I would be embarrassed to ask her, how many quilts she would need to make to become bored with making quilts. It just doesn't seem like the right question to ask. Maybe she would eventually become bored with quilts, and take up adjacent crafts such as embroidery.

Bernard Williams supposes that, were my mom immortal, there would come a time when all needlecraft would be a miserific tedium to her. He never asked her, but he's confident in his assertion because he thinks of human life most fundamentally in terms of desires to pursue various projects. You desire to do some things so you can go on doing other things. Williams calls these *conditional desires*. If you're like most people, you practice basic hygiene and do chores around the house not for their own sake but to foster good conditions for fulfilling more important

5. Cicero, *De finibus* 1.18.
6. Williams, "The Makropulos Case."

desires. These more important desires Williams calls *categorical desires*. These are the desires that are supposed to make life worth living.

Williams supposes that however strong your categorical desires, or however big or important are the projects they're aimed at, you'll eventually become intolerably bored by them.

It is hard not to dismiss Williams's argument as the putrescence of a sick flower of elite Western decadence, which uncritically thinks of life as structured by so many projects to be fulfilled. What will there be for me, a member of this elite class might wonder, after I've achieved my first-class degree at Oxford, or an Oxbridge fellowship, or a professorship, or a fellowship in the British Academy, or knighthood?

Few human beings think of their lives as a succession of opportunities for social and economic preferment. But there is a way of talking, considered normal among intellectually elite people who take Bernard Williams seriously, that divvies up the business of human living in terms of "projects." Raising kids, conducting a career, taking part in a political cause, pursuing a hobby, and so forth, are all conceptualized as so many projects. The thing about projects is that that they have beginnings, middles, and ends. If you are in sales, you meet with the client, draw up the bid, win the bid, and then deliver. At some point the project is over, at least for you: once the machines are installed and the invoice paid, your project is done, and now the project of customer service and maintenance begins for as long as the service contract stipulates. Your project might succeed, if you win all the way to the payment of the final invoice, or it might fail, if you can't get the meeting, or you don't win the bid, and so on.

But hardly any of what matters most in life is like this. Consider quilting. Making a single quilt is quite obviously a project, but the hobby of quilting is not. It is a sort of partial orientation of one's life around a craft. It is ongoing, with perhaps a clear beginning—Mom started quilting about twenty years ago—but no clear middle or ending. There is no sense to the thought of the project of quilting wrapping up. Sure, one might lose interest or become arthritic and unable to quilt, but these causes of the termination of quilting are no part of the craft of quilting as such.

Again, consider close relationships. Parents sometimes conceive of raising a kid as coming to an end, say, at high school or college graduation, or the kid leaving home for the first time, or getting married. And milestones like these really do seem to bring something to a close—childhood, let's say. But the relationship with one's offspring is or should be ongoing into adulthood. Not only is there little sense in conceiving close relationships as projects to be managed; there is also cringeworthy ignorance or perhaps willful perversion of what it means to be a parent, or a spouse, or a friend.

If the proper objects of our categorical desires really are projects, such that what is supposed to make life worth living is the conducting of various projects, then maybe we could begin to sympathize with Williams's assertion that immortal life, thus structured, would become intolerably boring and death a welcome relief. But if we focus instead on real life, which includes many projects but also includes a wide array of activities and states that can't meaningfully be construed as projects, then Williams's argument just fizzles out. Even if we accept for the sake of argument that having categorical desires is what makes life feel to me that it's worth living, it is difficult to imagine the frame of mind of a man who would think that the desire to continue a happy marriage or good friendship is the sort of desire that would inevitably be fulfilled in such a way as for the desire to come to an end.

Through real human relationships, eternal life beckons. Given our current constitution as mortals, we can acknowledge the wisdom of endings, the last communion, the final farewell and stirrup cup. But death is not a natural stopping point for the relationships we hold most dear. Nor for that matter is it a natural stopping point for other kinds of activities that are not projects: enjoying music, hiking, worshipping, reading. We know we could go on enjoying these forever were it not for death and the infirmities that precede it.

So, we must repudiate Williams's morbid thesis that even if immortality were possible, we should not want it. We do want it, not perhaps on any terms whatsoever, but if we imagine ourselves free from vices and all compulsive behavior, surrounded by people we love and who love us, healthy and painless, then yes, we would go on choosing immortality. And that is enough to keep us walking the ancient path with Lady Philosophy. We know the answer to Alphaville's question, do you really want to live forever and ever and ever? Yes.

And that *yes* implies a choice between despair and hope. If it really is impossible to get what we want, human life is fundamentally tragic. But if we cannot know it is impossible—that is, if for all we know it is possible, even if only remotely—then we can carry on in hope.

HOPE

I once gave a lecture to an academic audience on Thomas Aquinas's understanding of beatific vision, that supreme intellectual union with God that is, according to Aquinas, the supernatural end of every human being. I explained how, for Aquinas, human beings desire happiness above all but often disagree about how to achieve happiness. Like Boethius, Aquinas rejects the usual suspects of pleasure, wealth, prestige, power. In fact, *no created thing* can make a man truly happy. Aquinas of course believed in God, an infinite uncreated spirit with all power to elevate our mortal condition and make us fit for heaven, and so he could hope that the human yearning for beatitude was not fundamentally tragic.

A member of that audience was very unhappy with Aquinas and with me for sympathizing with Aquinas. "Why not think," she asked in that way academics ask questions when they really mean to make assertions, "that the real problem is with human desire? Isn't it the longing for a happiness that we cannot have that is the real source of our misery? If we could kill that desire, wouldn't we be free from suffering?"

Some readers will hereupon assume that this person is a Stoic. Or maybe a Buddhist. And she may well be, since her disquisition was an eloquent statement of the second of the Four Noble Truths of Buddhism. There is much that can be said in favor of that noble religion, but its fatal flaw is that it is beneath the dignity of man and woman to set our sights no higher than the absence of suffering. This is an essentially negative view of the good for human beings. The Thomistic and Boethian view is essentially positive, implying the absence of suffering but also the *presence* of virtue and joy.

There is little that can be said in defense of the positive vision against the negative vision to one already inclined to the negative vision. What I think can be said is this: whatever answers your reflective mind gives you about the reasonableness of hope or despair, of a negative or positive vision of the human good, your entire life physiologically and psychologically is *already* ordered by hope to the positive good. Remember, to pursue the human good is what we can't not do. Embracing a philosophy of hope is therefore simply to repeat in our professed philosophy what is already always going on as we get on with being humans. *Verso l'alto.*

Think about things that humans do. These show us that we in fact aim higher for ourselves than the absence of suffering. It may well be that a habit of getting out among the trees and flowers has anti-aging benefits, allowing us to live longer without pain than we otherwise would.[7] But only the health-and-wellness obsessed would take up the habit solely for that reason. Instead, people do it because it's fun, or beautiful, or awesome, or mysterious. We hike to enhance our lives, not to alleviate suffering, except as a byproduct. Here is a list of other things human do, some of which do indeed relieve suffering, but which are clearly not mere analgesics: painting, composing music, playing music, cooking a fancy meal, saying "I love you," reading a novel, studying philosophy, praying, writing poetry, restoring an old car, eating a candy bar, watching the sunset, waterskiing, painting one's fingernails, listening to music, reading poetry, landing a manned spacecraft on the surface of the moon, and so on.

Even many, maybe most, of the quotidian things we do not for their own sake but for the sake of something else—washing dishes, doing laundry, brushing teeth—seem ordered not merely to preventing or alleviating suffering but to dignifying, ennobling, our daily lives. Pigs feed, humans dine; and pigs neither set the table nor wash the dishes. Indeed, for human food, plates are practical, but upon reflection I think the use of washable porcelain plates causes my family and me more suffering than we'd have if we always used disposable paper plates. But we continue the hard human practice of washing the dishes because it is more dignified. Which is not to say that there is never a time or place for paper plates, for example the backyard on the Fourth of July, when we gather to do other odd human things that are more than mere pain relief: commemorate our founding and celebrate our country.

So one way to get, and remain, on the side of hope against despair, on the side of the positive pursuit of happiness against the negative avoidance of suffering, is to accept the sort of thing we are: strivers, metaphysical social climbers, cranky baby birds still in the nest, made for flight.

7. Kim et al., "Inequalities in Urban Greenness and Epigenetic Aging."

Another way is to attend carefully to an odd feature of Lady Philosophy's description of this perfect happiness that seems so out of reach. She frequently speaks of true happiness as though it were something *outside* a man, something *out there*, and if we could only get ourselves properly related to it, then we ourselves would have or be the happiness that it is.

People sometimes talk of history or the universe having things like arcs or sides. Famously, in a speech given at the Washington National Cathedral on March 31, 1968, just a few days before his assassination on April 4, Martin Luther King Jr. preached that the arc of the moral universe bends toward justice. Notice he does not say that human beings will gradually become more just or that together we humans will make the universe more just. Nor does he say that the universe will one day conform to our socially constructed notions of justice. All the action, he says, is out there: the moral universe stretched out through time past, long permitting atrocities, but racing ahead toward time future, with justice its inevitable terminus. It's as though he's imagining justice as a sort of force out there in the universe, not merely in human individuals and societies, and it is slowly conforming things to itself. That is meant as a comfort and a source of hope. That abstract intelligible thing, Justice, is not a mere word or a concept in someone's head. It is a real Force, and it will have its way.

Boethius, through Lady Philosophy, speaks of happiness in a similar way (C 3.9p). As we have seen, Lady Philosophy slowly builds up the definition of happiness, part by part. It—that is, happiness—is sufficient (*sufficientiam*) and powerful (*potentiam*). But then, she asks, isn't this thing, happiness, worthy of the highest honor (*veneratio*)? And if this thing, happiness, is sufficient and powerful and most worthy of honor, how could it fail to have the highest renown (*claritudo*)? And wouldn't the thing in possession of sufficiency, power, honor, and renown also have the fullness of joy (*laetitia*)?

Do you see what Lady Philosophy is up to? She is subtly, or perhaps not so subtly, equivocating between happiness as a quality that humans may or may not possess, and happiness as a thing out there, which is itself in possession of the attributes that make up the definition of happiness. On the one hand, "the true and complete happiness is the one that makes *a man* perfectly sufficient, powerful, revered, renowned, and joyful" (C 3.9p, 84). But on the other hand, happiness is *of all things* (*rerum omnium*) the most worthy of honor. This thing (*hoc*) is the most renowned. This thing (*hoc*) is the most joyful. And so on.

But there is a big difference between happiness considered as a quality that makes a man sufficient, powerful, etc., and happiness considered as the thing itself that is sufficient, powerful, etc.! What in the world is going on here? Happiness, it turns out, is God.

6

Happy God

"Do you think there is anything in these mortal, transitory affairs
that can bring about such a condition?"

"Not at all. You have demonstrated this well enough that no
further arguments are needed" (C 3.9p, 85).

This exchange marks a major transition in Lady Philosophy's
intervention. She has met a miserable man and freed him from
his inordinate attachment to the goods of fortune. Had she, or
Boethius, stopped here, we would have a *Consolation* that could
do little to console—a properly Stoic treatise. Learning that nothing in the world can make you truly happy puts you on a knife's
edge: on one side, a final abandonment of hope; on the other,
an opening of oneself to a transcendent hope. Lady Philosophy
had exhorted Boethius to abandon hope, as we saw in chapter 2.
But the hope she diagnosed as a disease was the fool's hope that
"these mortal, transitory affairs" can bestow beatitude. But now,
in pursuit of true consolation, she begins to prepare Boethius for
a new hope in a new object: the ultimate hope that reality is fundamentally good because willed into being and under the control
of God who is the Good.

Probably the most important night of my life was also my
most miserable. I was a young teenager who had been agonizing
over my bad fit with the cool kids at school. I had very normal

problems, though at the time I didn't know they were normal. I knew that I didn't have the right kind of clothes. I wondered, whenever I passed a tinted window, whether I looked weird when I walked. Despite my efforts, I could not easily use all the cuss words or make the dirty jokes. I could not enjoy the fashionable punk and rap music, again despite my efforts, because I was scandalized by their celebration of debauchery and violence. I obsessed over my apparent deficiencies. But that night it occurred to me, overwhelmingly, that life given over to these petty social worries was not a life worth living. Suddenly, it all seemed meaningless—not just teenage status-seeking but everything. My world went dark.

Then light broke in: a suggestion of purposefulness, a disclosure of benevolence. I lacked the concepts to think carefully about what I was experiencing, but as the moment passed, I identified it with God. Without articulating to myself a need to seek God, or even my ignorance about how to seek God, the thought occurred to me that I should go to church. A buddy at school had told me the year before how much he liked his church. My parents had taken my brother and me a handful of times to holiday services. Likely these experiences partially explain why church was the shape my pursuit of God took.

But the point of this story is not to recommend church. Instead, it's to associate my own story with the structure of Lady Philosophy's therapy: that opening to transcendent hope is most likely to occur only once we have given up on merely immanent hopes. The world is not enough, but many of us need a crisis to see this.

Recognizing that the happiness Lady Philosophy has defined is impossible to achieve exclusively through the goods of this world, Boethius turns his attention heavenward: "We should call upon the Father of all things" (C 3.9p, 85). Concurring, Lady Philosophy sings a prayer to God, God not as the Christians conceive him but—fittingly for Philosophy—as Plato conceived him in his dialogue *Timaeus*.[1]

Prayer often moves faster than reason, and this is fitting too, since our felt need for God outstrips what we can understand of God. Having finished her prayer, Lady Philosophy turns to the question of God's existence. She does not want Boethius to be "deceived by an ill-conceived image" (C 3.10p, 89). After all, perhaps only God can make us happy but there is no God. Then happiness would be impossible. Reality would be tragic. If we really could *know* there is no God, it would be right to dwell in that tragedy. But the upshot of Lady Philosophy's arguments is, at worst, that we cannot know that there is no God, and at best, that there is good reason to believe in God. And that belief, or even the belief in the *possibility* that God exists, is enough to nourish hope.

This strikes me as a pretty good reason not to be an atheist. Notice how low the commitment is at this point: to nourish a hope for happiness and avoid despair, all you need is an openness to God, a hopeful agnosticism rather than atheism.

Atheism was rather rare in the ancient world. It remains rare today, though those of us in the Western world encounter a disproportionate number of atheists relative to the whole human population. Given this blight of atheism, modern-day Boethians have all the more reason to offer reasons for God's existence.

Philosophers and theologians have made arguments for God for as long as there have been philosophers and theologians. Most of these arguments identify some feature of the world that cries out for explanation, and reason that only something transcending the world can explain that feature. For example, the order and intelligibility of the world suggest design, so there must be a designer.[2] Or, the evident objectivity of morality suggests a moral

1. Plato, *Timaeus* 27c.
2. Paley, *Natural Theology*.

law, so there must be a lawgiver.[3] Again, everything that can come into existence can do so only by a cause, and since there cannot be an infinite series of caused causes, there must be a first cause, uncaused.[4] And if you suppose that laws of nature explain the whole realm of things that can come into existence, there is still the need for a lawgiver—the laws don't explain themselves.[5] More recently, some philosophers have been impressed by the "fine-tuning" of our planet for the sort of complex life we have here on Earth, and reason that the existence of God makes it much more likely than the alternative that the universe would include such an anomalous life-teeming speck as planet Earth.[6] Some have found in our insatiable desire for happiness a reason for God: hunger suggests we are made to eat, even if some go hungry; so too human longing, not fully satisfiable by the familiar objects of desire, suggests we are made to enjoy something that transcends the world.[7] Others have thought that the very fact that we have an idea of God—infinite in perfection, so unlike every ordinary object of our experience—cries out for an explanation and that the best explanation is that God has given us the idea of himself, a sort of tracking device implanted in our minds to keep us searching for God amidst the destruction and confusion of the world.[8] Some have even argued for God on the grounds that there are *so many* good arguments for God![9]

These and many other arguments are developed with rigor elsewhere, and unsurprisingly each has its fair share of detractors as well as defenders. Boethius offers an additional route to God. To this we now turn.

---

3. Baggett and Walls, *Good God.*

4. Duns Scotus, *Treatise on the First Principle* 3; Aquinas, *Summa theologiae* 1.2.3.

5. Hildebrand and Metcalf, "The Nomological Argument."

6. Rota, "Why Is the Universe Just Right for Life?"

7. Buras and Cantrell, "A New Argument from Desire."

8. Descartes, *Meditations* 3.

9. Swinburne, *The Existence of God*; Poston, "The Argument from So Many Arguments."

GOD AND THE GOOD

Lady Philosophy's argumentative strategy is first to establish the existence of the Good, and then to reason from its existence to God's. Whether or not you find the argument cogent in the end, the argument is historically important, drawing on classical sources stretching back to Plato, while itself inspiring later philosophers such as Anselm (1033–1109) and John Duns Scotus (1265–1308). Here, we'll first examine Boethius's argument and then consider some of the sources that influenced it and that it influenced.

Recall from chapter 4 the foundational claim that everything seeks the good. Divergent as the various human efforts to pursue the good may be, we all pursue the good. In our pursuit of the good, we are not only similar to each other but similar to every other kind of thing: not only humans, but lions, songbirds, and trees (and, implicitly, all other types of things) pursue the good (C 1.2m). But it appears to be evident that the human good is not exactly the same as the lion's good, and neither is exactly the same as the songbird's, and so on.

So are there many different kinds of goodness—the human good, the leonine good, the avian good, and so on? Not quite. Or at least, not altogether different. There must be something that *unifies* these various types of good, despite their difference. After all, they are different types *of* good, not totally diverse kinds sharing nothing in common. So we look for goodness as such, or goodness itself, as that which unifies these different types of good. And what we should expect to find is that goodness itself is extremely saturated with intelligibility, so that it can in some mysterious sense hold within itself the human good, the leonine good, the avian good, and so on, for all the types of good. What is distinctive about the human good is not alien to goodness itself. It is not as though the human good is goodness *plus* some *additional features* that are no part of goodness itself. It is better to think of the human good as goodness itself *minus* whatever else about goodness happens not to pertain to the human good. Likewise for the other types of good.

Now, one obvious but important thing about goodness is that it comes in degrees (C 3.10p). Some things are better than others, not merely in the subjective sense that you prefer some things to other things, but in the objective sense that, regardless of your preferences, some things really and truly are better than other things. For example, a man who lies and cheats his way through life, enjoys doing so, and feels no remorse about it, is, in those respects, morally inferior to an honest and generous man. Given two runners who can run equally fast, the one with greater endurance is the better runner. Degrees of goodness hold even across kinds of things. A chimpanzee is objectively a better thing than a charcoal briquette, and a human being objectively better than a mosquito. There is no arguing for these claims; one sees them to be true and reasons in light of their truth, or one does not. Only knaves and fools fail to see their truth, or pretend to fail to see it.

When we make judgments about the degrees of goodness things have, we are making use of a concept of goodness. The concept functions as the standard or measure of our judgments. To judge one thing as better than another is to judge that it has more goodness than the other or perhaps that it more fully expresses goodness than the other. Now consider the concept of goodness. It is not the concept of this or that good thing but simply of the Good: pure, unsurpassable, unconditional, infinite goodness. By definition, nothing could be better than it. We might not be able to say much about it, but we employ it every time we make a judgment that something is good or that one thing is better than another.

The question, then, is whether the concept of the Good is the concept of anything *out there*, outside our thinking. This is a hard question. Here is, roughly, Boethius's answer. In our think-ing, the judgment that Fido is a good dog has three conceptual components: Fido, dog, and goodness. If we lacked these three concepts, we could not form the judgment that Fido is a good dog. This suggests an analogy to the real world: if, in the order of thought, there must be the concept of the Good in order to make the judgment that Fido is a good dog, why not think that, in the order of reality, there must really be the Good in order for Fido to be a good dog? If the analogy is good, then the Good exists, just as real as Fido (C 3.10p).

Not everyone will accept the analogy. Some claim to disbe-lieve that goodness really is out there in things and not just in our thinking about things. If they are reporting their beliefs cor-rectly (which I doubt), there is little hope for them. But others, acknowledging that goodness really is out there in things, nev-ertheless balk at the thought that the Good is there too. Perhaps the Good is merely a concept that we abstract from all the good things. If this is plausible, there is no need to suppose that there is the Good out there corresponding to our concept. I'm skeptical. If you're prepared to acknowledge the reality of good things, it seems to me an easy step to recognize the reality of the Good. But here we bump up against one of the oldest of philosophical debates. I cannot settle it one way or another; it is enough to state Boethius's side sympathetically.

From the reality of the Good, Boethius mounts an argument for God. God is the greatest thing imaginable (C 3.10p). Believ-ers and unbelievers alike can agree on this description, just as believers and unbelievers in Santa Claus can agree that Santa lives at the North Pole and wears a red suit. The point is that it's part of the concept of God that he is the greatest conceivable thing. Now, logically, the greatest conceivable thing either is good or is not good. But obviously something that is not good cannot be the greatest conceivable being. So, it is good. Again, logically, the greatest conceivable thing either is unsurpassably good or it is not. But obviously something that is surpassable in goodness is not the greatest conceivable thing. So it is unsurpassably good. But the Good is, by definition, that which is unsurpassably good. And it has already been granted that the Good exists. So the Good either is God or is in God. So if the Good is God then God exists. And if the Good is in God, God exists, since an existing thing cannot be in a nonexisting thing. Therefore, God exists (C 3.10p).

Here is why we should think that the Good is not somehow *in* God but *just is* God (C 3.10p). If God has the Good as a part or a property, then there is some sort of real distinction between God and the Good. But then God would depend for his goodness on his possession of the Good: it would be due to possessing the Good and not to his very nature that he is good. But God is the greatest conceivable being, and it is greater to be good by nature than to be good by possessing goodness. Therefore, God is good by nature. Therefore, God is the same as the Good.

INFLUENCE AND DEVELOPMENT

The deepest influence on Boethius's rational route to God is Plato. Plato's Socrates said in his pious discourse on the Good, "Any measure of such things that falls short in any way of that which is is not good measure, for nothing incomplete is the measure of anything."[10] But a more direct influence likely comes from an argument attributed to Cleanthes (331–231 BC), Zeno's first successor as head of the Stoic school.

Cleanthes reasoned that if one nature is better than another, there must be a nature that is the best. To see this, suppose one nature is indeed better than another, but there is no nature that is best. Then for any nature that is better than another, there is yet another that is better than it. But then there would be an infinite

10. Plato, *Republic* 6 504c.

series of natures. Such an infinite series is impossible. Therefore, there is a nature that is best. God is by definition the best nature. Therefore, God exists.[11]

Another likely influence on Boethius is the great Augustine, who, as far as I am aware, was the first to formulate explicitly the thought that God is not merely the "best nature," as Cleanthes put it, but the greatest *conceivable* thing. God, according to Augustine, is "that than which nothing better can exist or be conceived" (*quo esse aut cogitari melius nihil possit*).[12]

But the most famous argument for God that is similar to Boethius's was developed centuries later by Anselm, an argument commonly described as the "ontological argument." God, says Anselm, is by definition "that than which nothing greater can be conceived." God "exists in the intellect," which is to say that we have a coherent concept of God. Now suppose God exists *only* in the intellect—that is, suppose God is not real. Then we could conceive something greater than God—namely, something that had all the great features of God with the added benefit of being real. But this is absurd, since God by definition is the greatest conceivable being. Therefore, God really exists, not just in the intellect.[13]

Anselm's development of Boethius's argument has earned him first mention in histories of the ontological argument, and probably rightfully so since the earlier efforts in Boethius and Cleanthes are not as fully developed as Anselm's.

Many versions of the argument have been developed since Anselm. One of the best comes from Duns Scotus. According to Scotus, part of what it means to be the greatest conceivable being is to be unable to be caused. Possibly, the greatest conceivable being exists—that is, the concept of the greatest conceivable being is

11. Sextus Empiricus, *Against the Physicists* 1, in *Selections from the Major Writings*, 196; Sandbach, *The Stoics*, 69–70.

12. Augustine, *De Moribus* 2.11.24, in Migne, ed., PL 32, col. 1355.

13. Anselm, *Proslogion* 2.

a coherent concept. Suppose the greatest conceivable being does not exist. Then it cannot exist, since by nature it is unable to be caused, and nothing can begin to exist without being caused to exist. But it can exist. Therefore, it does exist. God is the greatest conceivable being. Therefore, God exists.[14]

More recently, the contemporary philosopher Alvin Plantinga (b. 1932) offered a new version of the argument, inspired by Saul Kripke's (1940–2022) "possible worlds" semantics of modal logic. Kripke's theory stipulates that what it means for something to be *possible* is that it exists in some possible world. Likewise, to be *necessary* is to exist in every possible world. Our own world is the possible world that happens to be the *actual* world. So if something really or actually exists, it exists in the actual world. Now, part of what it is to be God is to be a necessary being. So if God exists, he exists in every possible world. And if God does not exist, he exists in no possible world. But it is possible that God exists. So, God exists in a possible world. Therefore, God exists in all possible worlds, including the actual world. Therefore, God exists.[15]

Unsurprisingly, not everyone is persuaded by ontological arguments—"unsurprisingly" because no philosophical argument ever persuades everyone. The earliest critic was actually a contemporary of Anselm's, a monk named Gaunilo. He offered a parody of Anselm's argument that goes roughly like this: The Golden Isle is the greatest conceivable island. It exists in the intellect. Suppose that it does not really exist. Then we can imagine a greater—namely, the island with all the features of the Golden Isle with the added benefit of really existing. But this is absurd since the Golden Isle by definition is the greatest conceivable island. Therefore, the Golden Isle really exists. Notice that Gaunilo's parody doesn't say exactly what's supposed to be wrong with Anselm's

14. Duns Scotus, *Treatise on the First Principle* 4.79(65).
15. Alvin Plantinga, *God, Freedom, and Evil*, 108–12.

original. The point seems to be that it's clearly ludicrous to suppose we can establish the existence of such an island by means of this sort of reasoning. So it must be equally ludicrous to establish God's existence this way.[16]

The problem with Gaunilo's parody, however, is with the second premise stated above: that the Golden Isle exists in the intellect. It does no such thing. To see this, remember that to exist in the intellect means merely that a concept is coherent. But the concept of the greatest conceivable island is incoherent. So it does not exist in the intellect. Therefore, it does not exist in reality. Here's how we know the concept of the greatest conceivable island is incoherent: for something to be an *island*, it must be made of land and surrounded by water. But for anything like this we can always imagine a bigger and better. But it is not like this with God. The concept of the greatest conceivable *being* has no limits. It is not by nature made of land, or surrounded by water, or subject to anything that would render it unable to be unsurpassable. So Gaunilo's parody fails to refute Anselm's argument.[17]

Of course, there are other objections, and other replies to those objections. Philosophers have been discussing Anselm's argument for nearly a thousand years! But again, the point here is not to attempt a final word for or against Anselm's or Boethius's arguments, or any of the other arguments in their vicinity, but rather to present them in a sympathetic way and hopefully inspire you to grapple with them on your own.

GOD, HAPPINESS, AND UNITY

Lady Philosophy's identification of God with the Good permits one of the odder and most delightful inferences in all of philosophical thought about God: if we always seek the good, and

16. Gaunilo, "Reply on Behalf of the Fool," in Anselm, *Basic Writings*, 99–104.
17. Anselm, "Reply to Gaunilo," in *Basic Writings*, 105–14.

if the good we all seek is happiness, and if God is the Good, it follows that God is happiness.

It also follows that the Good we all seek is God. But these two inferences seem to be in tension with each other. Happiness and God sure seem like two different things. Sure, we can acknowledge the religious commonplace that only God can make us happy. But this does not require that God *is* happiness; it only requires that God is the *source* of happiness. But Boethius says something stronger. He takes for granted that God is the source of happiness. But he is emphatic: *God is happiness* (C 3.10p).

At the level of logic, it's not hard to see how Boethius gets here. Recall: Everything seeks the good, not only humans but every other type of thing. The goods for all the types of things have a unity in their diversity: despite the fact that the human good is not exactly the same as the leonine or avian good, there is something these goods share in common, the Good itself. When we say that the human good is happiness, we identify what it is about the Good that is perfective of human nature. The identification of the Good with happiness, therefore, does not rule out the identification of the Good with other ways in which it is perfective of other natures. Whatever the leonine good is, the Good is that too. And so, God is that too. Likewise for human nature. Its good is happiness; the Good is that. And so too is God.

But even if we can follow the sequence of logical inferences, there is still something jarring about the claim that God is happiness. Maybe this is because we have too stern an image of God fixed in our minds, from bad teaching or by projecting the imperfections of our earthly parents and leaders onto God. Maybe it's because we associate happiness too closely with feelings or moods and somehow recognize that God's emotional life, or whatever analogue of emotional life he has, is bound to be rather unlike ours.

Yet, recalcitrant as these hang-ups may be, I think we can make some progress here. Anyone who has been overwhelmed by a great love or a great beauty is familiar with the experience sometimes described as being taken outside of oneself, or of losing oneself. For just a moment, the object of desire or adoration *is* your joy, not the *source* of your joy. Colloquial English captures a little of this experience: it is common to call the one you love *my love, my dear, my heart's desire*. In doing so, we are not merely saying that she is the one I love or the one I hold dear or the one my heart desires. We are saying that she is my love, my dear, my desire. She has drawn the lover outside himself, so that his love for her somehow is her.

This, I think, is a little of what's going on in Boethius's identification of God with happiness—a mystical strand in his thought, woven around the syllogisms. To become attuned to God as the source of all good things and as unsurpassably good, inspires just that sort of being taken outside of oneself that great love or beauty inspires. God is not just the *source* of his happiness, but *is* happiness.

And if this is right, or on the right track, it goes some way toward resolving the old tension between *eros* and *agape*. *Eros* is the love that seeks to possess the beloved, whereas *agape* is the love that wills what is good for the beloved, for the beloved's own sake. When the lover is taken outside of himself in love, identifying his love with the beloved, it no longer makes sense to describe his love as merely self-interested (*eros*) or merely disinterested (*agape*). He acts for her sake (*agape*) and, in doing so, fulfills his desire (*eros*).

The identification of happiness with God also permits a stronger explanation of the unity of happiness that Lady Philosophy had offered earlier. As discussed in chapter 5, she had argued that the various aspects of happiness—sufficiency, honor, influence, fame, pleasure—are really one and the same because they are interdependent: you can't fully have one without having all the others. But if happiness is God, the unity of these aspects of happiness is much tighter, not mere interdependence but something more like identity. This strange thought is a little less strange when we recall, again from chapter 5, that these various goods we all seek as we seek the Good are "images of happiness."

Strictly speaking, sufficiency, honor, influence, fame, and pleasure are not five parts or pillars of happiness but are diverse images of one and the same thing, happiness. Imagine five portraits of one and the same person, done by different artists in their distinctive styles. Each portrait expresses its subject a little differently, so we learn more about the subject by studying all five than we would by studying just one. But through these five, we are learning about just one thing, the subject.

Turns out, as Lady Philosophy initiates Boethius deeper into the theological core of her consolation, that these five types of goods are images of the Good, and that the reality we seek when we seek good things under any of these types is the one Good. Only as unified in their source and exemplar are these goods really the Good we seek (C 3.11p).

Have you ever been caught up in some pursuit, fully in the zone, distraction-free, only to come out of it with a kind of nostalgia for all the normal things in life you've temporarily ignored? A project at work, for example, or an engrossing novel. Nothing else seems to matter, until it does again. Then things like hanging out with friends or cooking your own food or taking a long hot shower suddenly seem immensely attractive. It's as though we want to make up for ignoring these other good parts of life.

We all have an idealized vision of "normal life," and while its precise contours differ for each of us, what is common to our visions is a kind of balance or harmony of the various tasks we need and want to do. We have our bodies to take care of, our relationships and leisure to enjoy, our work to do, and so on, and we want all these to fit together so that, as little as possible, none is pursued at the cost of any of the others. We all recognize how hard this unity is to maintain, but we long for it.

These, I think, are some helpful ways to appreciate Lady Philosophy's linking of our desire for happiness with a desire for unity. Only the simple live balanced lives. God alone enjoys the truly simple life. Our own thwarted—often self-thwarted—pursuit of an integrated or unfragmented life attests both to our desire for the simple God and to the impossibility of finding the unity we seek in this world of entropy and metabolism. Boredom is not caused by too little activity but too much. We have too much to do.

This explains, in a purely natural way, why practices of prayer or meditation are so important. To do these well is not only to be free of distraction but to be fully present in the moment—not in the merely colloquial sense of paying attention but the literal sense of having all of oneself engaged. When I pray, I sometimes realize that I am doing the best thing I know how to do, which is just what Jesus taught his disciples to do.[18] Look to the deepest source of your being (Our Father, who art in heaven, hallowed be thy name). Ask for the harmony and simplicity of heaven to be manifest here below (thy kingdom come, thy will be done, on earth as it is in heaven). Elaborate that request by connecting the needs of your body with your relationship with God (give us this day our daily bread); by confessing the need for God's help in restoring your imperfect relationships with God and those around you (forgive us our trespasses as we forgive those who trespass against us); and by asking for continual assistance to avoid whatever is incompatible with the happiness you truly seek (lead us not into temptation, but deliver us from evil). Prayer, by this template or others, is the unifying activity *par excellence*, uniting us with the simple God and, thereby, bringing unity to our fragmented selves.

18. Matthew 6:9–13.

DIVINIZATION

There is at present a best-selling book of the sort business travelers buy in airport terminals. It is called *Homo Deus*, by Yuval Noah Harari, and it is a world-class fever dream of techno-mysticism. The human longing for God is the human longing to be God. And we are at the threshold of realizing that desire by means of our amazing technologies.

There are many things to say in criticism of Harari's book, but here are two. First, there is an obvious equivocation here about the meaning of "God." I am prepared to admit that various technologies might give some people (the rich) ominous physical and computational advantages over the unenhanced masses. That this is a sincere, if not ultimate, desire of many in the Davos or Silicon Valley set, I have little doubt. But to equate these advantages with the achievement of divinity is laughable not just to those who know the rudiments of Christian theology but to anyone vaguely aware of Homer or Hesiod. Second, Harari's depiction of the point of religious life has far more in common with magicians like Doctor Faustus than mystics like St. John of the Cross or St. Thérèse of Lisieux—and we all know whom Faustus called on to get what he wanted.

And yet—I'll repeat the words to express a begrudgingly conciliatory attitude—and yet, in Harari we have a faint echo of the Boethian theme that our pursuit of happiness is one and the same as our pursuit of God. Lady Philosophy makes it explicit: "Since men become blessed from the acquisition of blessedness, and blessedness is indeed divinity, it is clear that men become blessed through the acquisition of divinity. . . . Men who have acquired divinity become gods. Each blessed man is therefore a god" (C 3.10p, 90). The gospel according to Boethius is that the apotheosis reserved in pagan antiquity for heroes like Hercules is available to all men, if only they would be happy.

Again, at the level of pure logic, the inferences are unavoidable: God is identical with happiness; therefore, to increase in happiness is to increase in divinity. To the extent we are happy, we are divine. But again, it is one thing to follow the logic and another to understand what Boethius is really driving at. On its face, the claim that we become gods by becoming happy is absurd. It smacks of the same equivocation about "god" of which Harari is guilty.

But I think there is more going on here. One thing about great love is its power to unify the lover with the beloved: "I am my beloved's and my beloved is mine."[19] "All my worldly goods, I thee endow," as it says in the order for matrimony in the old Anglican *Book of Common Prayer*.[20] To draw nearer to God is a little bit like this (endowed with heavenly goods, so to speak), becoming more like him, more able to enjoy what he enjoys and to do as he does: more *unified, at one*, in will and action.

Mystics sometimes speak of losing oneself in God or becoming one with God.[21] We must take them seriously; but we must also not blaspheme. It is impermissible to construe talk of mystical union as ceasing to exist. When I eat a cheeseburger, for a while I am united with it. But once I've digested it, it makes no sense to say I am one with the cheeseburger, for there is no longer a cheeseburger to be one with. Just so, whatever radical union has been experienced by those overwhelmed by the loving presence of God, they continue to exist, however transformed and however united with God.

This is a paradox of religious life. St. Paul said, "It is no longer I who live, but Christ who lives in me."[22] And also, "You have died,

19. Song of Songs 6:3.

20. *The Book of Common Prayer*, 1662 ed., 304.

21. Bernard of Clairvaux, "On Loving God" 10.28, in *Selected Works*; John of the Cross, "Song of the Soul and the Bridegroom" 18–20, and "Song of the Soul that Rejoices" 5–8, in *Selected Poems*.

22. Galatians 2:20.

and your life is hid with Christ in God."[23] At the most extreme literal reading of these texts, we fall into absurdities. If Paul has died, then Christ is the one writing that letter. But then Christ is lying, because he identifies himself in the letter as Paul. Again, if we have died and our lives are hidden in Christ, why does Paul bother to speak to us? Or why doesn't he address Christ instead?

So, we must avoid the extreme literal reading. And yet there is nearly as much danger in not reading these texts literally enough. The danger is that we persist in one of the great anthropological errors of our time, the error of the atomized, autonomous self. There is something about the language of death or annihilation that really should tune us in to the reality of union with and dependence on God. Human life—all of it, body, soul, mind, and strength—is designed to receive and to convey divine life.

There is something rational about Egyptian worship of the sun, both the monotheistic sun worship introduced by Akhenaten and even the standard polytheistic worship of Ra as king of gods. This is because sun worship implies recognition of the way in which our organic lives are utterly dependent on the light and energy of the sun. It is the sun's power in me and around me that enables me to see and to move and to nourish myself. Just so, it is God's power in me, conveyed through the sun and many other channels, that sustains my being.

The mystical experience of becoming one with God is, I suggest, something like an affirming recognition in one's deepest self of that total dependence on divine activity that already obtains simply by virtue of the fact that one exists. You are, already, shot through with God's energy—God living in and through you. It is the quest of religious life to recognize and welcome that fact in every aspect of life. Since we have a congenital resistance both to that recognition and to that welcome, achieving these is a sort of death, a losing or abandoning of oneself. Thankfully, the

23. Colossians 3:3.

experience of profound earthly love or beauty, in which we identify our deepest desires not with ourselves but with the beloved,
gives us a hint that dying to self and living with and for God,
however difficult to achieve, is not wholly alien to the sort of life
we already have.

For all its logical support, I cannot understand Boethius's
claim that we are gods to the extent we are happy apart from this
mystical background. No matter how happy we get, we simply
don't become God. It is absurd to think otherwise, since part of
what it is to be God is to be uncaused and eternal, and nothing
can *become* uncaused and eternal. But there is a way in which
Harari can achieve his heart's desire: not through technology but
through the joyfully hard pursuit of godliness. "When I wake up
after thy likeness, I shall be satisfied with it."[24]

And here, finally, Lady Philosophy tells Boethius what he really is: not merely a "rational and mortal creature," as he had said
of himself in his stupor when she first asked him what he is, but
a person made to share in the divine life. "This is beautiful and
priceless," he tells her (C 3.10p, 92).

24. Psalm 17:16 (Book of Common Prayer, 1662 ed.).

7

Evil as Privation

PROVIDENCE

The potential for divinization is the part of the definition of man Boethius could not supply when Lady Philosophy first asked what sort of thing he was (C 1.6p). She has brought him very far indeed, from a man complaining that death had not come for him to a man cherishing a hope that he will grow into a god.

In *Paradiso*, the third and final part of the *Divine Comedy*, Dante's beloved Beatrice guides him through the heavenly spheres on their way to a beatifying vision of God. But long before that final vision, Dante requires periodic power boosts to continue his progress through heaven. The most memorable of these boosts occurs almost immediately upon entry. He gazes upward but is blinded by the sun. The light was so bright it seemed that God had "adorned the heavens with a second sun."[1] He's not ready for that sort of light. So he turns his gaze instead to Beatrice, who reflects heaven's double sunlight. Beholding her, he is, as he puts it, *transhumanized*, made like a god, and, so empowered, his senses adjust to their divine environment. When he finally wins through to the end, he seems to enjoy that unity with God of which the mystics speak: "All my will and my desires / turned . . . by / The Love that moves the sun and the other stars."[2]

1. Dante, *Paradise* 1.63, trans. Esolen, 7.
2. Dante, *Paradise* 33.143–45, trans. Esolen, 359.

120

Dante's report of his experience discloses something about himself and something about everything else: it took him a journey through hell, purgatory, and heaven for his will and desires to achieve *what already obtains* throughout the cosmos. He explains the orderly motions of the heavenly bodies not through laws of nature but through the love of God. We need not fault him here for being unscientific, for ultimately there is no incompatibility between a theological and a merely natural account of natural phenomena. To put the point somewhat blandly, that the natural world behaves with law-like regularity is the sort of fact that cries out for explanation, and a theological explanation of that fact is the sort of explanation that is ultimate: it explains everything else but itself has no need of explanation.

Like Dante, Boethius associates his movement toward God with the movement of the whole world of nature. It seems necessary, he says, that there should be some single organizing and guiding principle of the whole universe. The unity and order of the universe seem inexplicable without ultimate recourse to an uncaused first cause that is the one and the same cause of everything in the universe (C 3.12p).

Lady Philosophy agrees but tries to illumine for Boethius the manner in which God guides the universe. "Providence" is that term theologians use to describe God's benevolent governance of all things. But just as a donkey may be controlled with a stick or a carrot, so too there are several logically possible ways God might be said to govern the universe. One way, more like the stick, is simply to exert top-down control over everything or—to change the metaphor—to keep everything in the world on puppet strings. But this is not the way Lady Philosophy imagines God's providence. Instead, more like the carrot, she imagines God as the Good and so the ultimate universal object of desire (C 3.12p). Merely natural things, things other than persons, seek the Good by nature, each in its own distinctive way. But the wild variety of natural tendencies converges on one and the same Good. The unity of the Good explains the unity of nature, its orderliness and predictability, while the goodness of the Good explains the goodness of nature, its harmony and beauty.

But the carrot theory does not provide a complete account of providence. After all, things like us possess freedom over our thinking and acting. Even if we can't help but do everything we do ultimately for the Good, it remains that it is possible for us to do what we know to be bad or stupid. And the ability to seek the Good badly seems to imply the possibility of failing to achieve the Good. Consider: I may have a firmly fixed desire to drive my car to Dallas. But if I put water in my gas tank, I will fail to fulfill this desire. So, our firmly fixed natural tendency to seek the Good is not adequate for explaining how our bad actions fall under God's providential rule.

Thus, there is more to the story about providence. As Lady Philosophy puts it, "There is not anything that would *either* want *or* be able to resist this highest Good" (C 3.12p, 103). The point of the either/or is this: insofar as things act in accordance with their natures, they tend toward the Good. But it is possible, at least for free people, to act in discord with their natures. To act discordantly with one's nature is to be opposed to God. But nothing can successfully oppose God. God ensures that even acts of rebellious discord harmonize, eventually, with his good universe. (There is even more to the story of providence, as we will see in chapter 9, but this is enough for now.)

In the grand cosmology in the background of Tolkien's beloved story, *The Lord of the Rings*, the one God Eru creates a variety of spiritual beings, rather like angels or gods. Eru propounds a theme of music and bids his angels sing. Their song is beautiful until Melkor, the most powerful spirit in the choir, decides he wants to make his own music, out of sync and discordant with Eru's. Twice, Eru intervenes with a second and then a third theme to drown out Melkor's braying, but Melkor just sings on, his music "loud, and vain," like many trumpets repeating a few notes. Melkor's music aimed "to drown the other music by the violence of its voice." But Melkor's efforts could not succeed. We're told that "the most triumphant notes" of his music were woven into the "solemn pattern" of Eru's third theme.

Finally, Eru has had enough. He silences the music and rebukes his wayward angel: "Thou, Melkor, shalt see that no theme may be played that hath not its uttermost source in me, nor can any alter the music in my despite. For he that attempteth this shall prove but mine instrument in the devising of things more wonderful, which he himself hath not imagined."[3]

Eventually, Eru makes their music visible and shows his spirits a vision of a world. Somehow, they can see in the vision the shape of their distinctive contributions. And to Melkor, Eru offers a second rebuke: "Thou, Melkor, wilt discover all the secret thoughts of thy mind, and wilt perceive that they are but a part of the whole and tributary to its glory."[4]

To see Lady Philosophy's full account of providence, we ought to imagine something like Melkor's efforts against Eru. As a free and powerful agent, Melkor's bad deeds really do make a difference to the world. Yes, they mar and corrupt. Yet Eru will ensure that all of Melkor's bad deeds accomplish good ends, thereby ensuring Melkor's total frustration.

God exercises providence, then, *both* as the universal object of desire *and* as the benevolent ruler who harmonizes everything, even bad deeds, with goodness. Carrot as the default, stick when necessary.

---

3. Tolkien, *Silmarillion*, 6.
4. Tolkien, *Silmarillion*, 6.

THE PROBLEM OF EVIL

One of the dispositions of the philosopher is a willingness to flounder a bit in search of answers to hard questions. Another is a tendency to be proactive about searching out the hard questions, seeking objections to one's preferred or even cherished theories. Add to these dispositions persistence and honesty, and you have the makings of a true philosopher.

Lady Philosophy models these dispositions. Having heard her discourse on providence, Boethius is euphoric, all his concerns for the moment assuaged. But this is Philosophy's clinic, and she won't let her patient rest when there are important objections to consider. Imagine it: Boethius is in prison waiting to die. Lady Philosophy has come and taught him the hope of God and he is happy. But she does not want him naive, to nourish only a fool's hope. She risks his newfound comfort by pressing him to think harder.

"Now do you want us to bring our ideas together into conflict? . . . Perhaps from such a collision some beautiful spark of truth might fly forth" (C 3.12p, 104).

To bring ideas into conflict is to entertain the possibility that you have inconsistent beliefs. You consider the beliefs side by side, so to speak, trying to identify their logical relationship: consistent or inconsistent? Where there is some reason to think the pair might fall short of consistency, the engine of philosophy revs to life, making distinctions, posing counterexamples, raising objections, following arguments, all in pursuit of a responsible judgment about whether the apparent inconsistency is real or merely apparent.

Philosophy's first allegiance is to the truth, and the thing about inconsistent beliefs is that *at most* one is true. This means a firm judgment that your beliefs are inconsistent rationally requires you to *reject* at least one of them. Where the beliefs are about things that really matter to you, the prospect of rejecting any of them is and should be unsettling, daunting even. Your little philosophical exercise might, if you let it, lead to a complete upheaval of your way of life.

In the narrative of *Consolation*, Boethius of course accepts Lady Philosophy's invitation to bring their ideas into conflict. But what ensues is deeply troubling to him. This conflict of ideas forces him to wrestle with some of the hardest issues in philosophy: the problem of evil and whether free will is real or just an illusion. But however troubling Boethius finds the philosophical effort to maintain the consistency of his beliefs, he never backs down.

We have heard many beautiful and sublime things about God and the extravagant hope God undergirds: the possibility of becoming gods and the providential goodness or making good of all things. But these beautiful thoughts are threatened by the inescapable fact of evil. At first glance, the kinds and scope of the evils we commit and suffer do not seem consistent with all the beautiful thoughts about God and providence. It seems that one of these has got to go, and however much we would prefer to keep the God stuff and jettison the evil, the evil is obvious and God is debatable. Therefore, it is God that has to go.

Lady Philosophy lays out the problem differently, exasperatingly: God can do everything, right? Yes, of course. But God can't do evil, right? No, of course he can't. Well, then, "evil is nothing . . . since the one who can do everything is unable to do it" (C 3.12p, 104). Boethius's reaction to this apparently glib sophistry is exactly what ours should be: "Are you toying with me and turning me around in an impossible maze of logic?" (C 3.12p, 104). She avers she is not toying with him, but simply drawing out an inference from premises they already agree on. She is saying, in effect, that given the conflict between God and evil, it is evil that has to go. More precisely, we need to revise our understanding of what evil is, to make sense of how it can manifest in a world under the good care of God.

The philosopher who has grasped the reality of God is like Orpheus overcoming hell to win back his beloved Eurydice. Hades lets them go on one condition: Orpheus must not turn back to look at Eurydice on their escape from hell. If he does, she will be lost forever. But he cannot resist. He looks back, and she is lost forever. "This story is for you," Lady Philosophy sings, "for those who wish to lead / the mind into the upper day. / Since, whoever, having been weakened, turns back a gaze to Tartarus's chasm— / whatever excellence he has gained, / looking back, he loses" (C 3.12m, 104).

The song is an encouragement to Boethius not to doubt what they have already achieved in their dialectical back and forth but to keep pressing on, following the arguments wherever they lead. The wickedness of the world is a powerful temptation to toss those arguments aside. But in doing so, Boethius would lose a treasure greater even than Eurydice. Do not be afraid to draw the inference: given all we've established about God and providence, evil must not be the force our fear or sorrow make it out to be. There is a lot of work yet to be done to show all this, but don't abort the honest philosophical quest the moment it faces a challenge.

PRIVATION THEORY OF EVIL

It is common to use subhuman epithets to describe people who fail to live up to the norms of being human: brute, beast, pig, wolf in sheep's clothing, dog, cur, chicken, flighty, bird-brained, monkey mind, snake, cold fish, jackass. Implicit in this linguistic practice is the belief that the human form of life is better, nobler, than the forms of life of the beasts, and that the mere fact of being human bestows the obligation not to live like the beasts, such that to act like a pig or a chicken or a jackass is to act badly.

The boy-hero Curdie, in George MacDonald's (1824–1905) *The Princess and Curdie*, is given the gift to discern the true character of whomever he meets simply by shaking their hands. The princess who bestows the gift explains, "All men, if they do not take care, go down the hill to the animals' country; . . . many men are actually, all their lives, going to be beasts. People knew it once, but it is long since they forgot it. . . . Since it is always what they do, whether in their minds or their bodies, that makes men go down to be less than men, that is, beasts, the change always comes first in their hands—and first of all in the inside hands, to which the outside ones are but as the gloves. . . . Hence of course it follows that you will be able often, and with further education in zoology, will be able always to tell, not only when a man is growing a beast, but what beast he is growing to, for you will know the foot—what it is and what beast's it is. According, then, to your knowledge of that beast will be your knowledge of the man you have to do with."[5]

The princess told Curdie that people once knew that by becoming bad we become like beasts, but that we have forgotten. The princess was right. Homer knew: remember Circe, who transformed Odysseus's overindulgent sailors into pigs.[6] And Epictetus wrote that the vicious become like animals: those who are deceptive, cunning, and pernicious are like wolves; the fierce, brutal, and wild are like lions; a scurrilous and malicious person is like a fox, or else "some lower and more wretched creature. "So be careful, and make sure that you don't turn out to be one of these wretched creatures."[7]

Boethius agrees. The covetous man is like a wolf; the wild, restless, litigious man is like a dog; the deceptive man like a little

5. MacDonald, *The Princess and Curdie*, 68.
6. Homer, *Odyssey* 10.
7. Epictetus, *Discourses* 1.3, in *The Complete Works*, trans. Waterfield, 77.

fox; the timid is like a deer; the sluggish like an ass; the fickle a bird; and the lustful a pig (C 4.3p).

I encourage you not to write these warnings off as mere fantasy. We cannot take them literally, but we should take them seriously. The image of the man who becomes a beast is a helpful way to grasp the counterintuitive view about evil that is the core of Boethius's response to the problem of evil.

The view is that evil is always and only the privation of goodness. The word "privation" is roughly the same as "lack" but has a connotation "lack" does not. A privation is a lack where a lack *should not be*. Both the blind man and the stone have the same lack: neither can see. But inability to see is not a privation in the stone precisely because stones are not the sorts of things by nature suited to see. By contrast, a man is the sort of thing by nature suited to see, so when a man is blind, we rightly judge that he lacks a power he should have. His blindness is not merely a *lack* of sight but a *privation* of sight.

So, if a privation is a lack where a lack should not be, the privation theory of evil says that *evil is a lack of goodness where goodness should be*. If a man is a lyin' cheatin' scoundrel through and through, we can say he lacks the virtues of honesty and justice. There are other kinds of things that lack these virtues: a celery stick, for example, has no honesty or justice. Neither does a clothes hanger, blast it. Down with all daffodils, for they have no honesty or justice! But upon reflection, it is no fault of the celery or hanger or daffodil to lack honesty and justice, because these aren't the kinds of things that can have moral virtues. But people are. So, the dishonest and unjust man deserves our opprobrium, and the celery does not. The lack of honesty and justice in these inanimate things is merely a lack; but the lack of these virtues in a man is more than a lack: it is a privation.

Boethius invites us to see all evils as privations. Given the intensity of our suffering, it sometimes feels irresistible to attribute positive reality to evil, like the dark side of the Force in the *Star Wars* universe. But Boethius offers a less mysterious, more reasonable alternative: evil is not a positive force but a privation.

The privation theory of evil makes sense of a common way of using the word "bad." A bad apple is an apple that has gone bad—that is, it has lost the features that make it good for eating. A bad film is a film that is seriously deficient in the qualities that make for good films. The badness is not something added to these but something subtracted. A hole in a blanket is where the blanket is not. A hole in a plot is where plot should be but isn't. More generally, "bad" only makes sense as an evaluative term given some ideal or standard compared to which the bad thing falls short. I think the same should be said about "evil." We tend to reserve this word for people, or for things that happen to people, and not for inanimate objects. But the same point holds: an evil person is a person who seriously lacks the good qualities a person should have.

But here is an important caveat. A virtue like justice is the sort of thing that can be acquired only after a decent amount of living. It makes little sense to describe an infant as having the virtue of justice. So the baby lacks justice. But we don't fault her for it. She's not yet of the age to have acquired any virtues. We do fault the full-grown man for his lack of justice, precisely because a full-grown man should be just. Thus, while the baby and the man are equally people, the immaturity of the baby makes it morally unproblematic that she lacks justice, whereas the maturity of the man makes his lack of justice morally problematic. So, too, an unripe apple is not a bad apple.

On the privation theory of evil, goodness is the real and primary thing; evil or badness the corruption of the good. Darkness is the absence of light; coldness the absence of heat. The orcs seem to be evil through and through, but they are actually corruptions of the elves. The dark lord, we are told, cannot create anything off his own bat; he can only twist and mar what is originally good.[8]

I often think about a literary inversion of the truth that darkness is the absence of light. The wanderer Anodos in Mac-Donald's *Phantastes* finds himself in the cottage of an ogress. As he stumbles in, she is reading from a book, and this is what she reads: "The light doth but hollow a mine out of the infinite extension of the darkness. And ever upon the steps of the light treadeth the darkness; yea, springeth in fountains and wells amidst it, from the secret channels of its mighty sea. Truly, man is but a passing flame, moving unquietly amid the surrounding rest of night, without which he yet could not be, and whereof he is in part compounded."[9]

I try to imagine the darkness as the primary thing and the light merely as the absence of darkness. I cannot quite do it. What I find when I try is that I'm not really thinking about darkness but about something black, like a great piece of black felt or foam or a great black blanket. Then, it is easy to think of light as a sort of color disrupting the black monochrome. But that is not really to imagine light as the absence of darkness; it's to imagine a mostly black thing with some white or yellow on it.

I think this way about evil too. Once you get firmly in mind the distinction between a mere lack and a privation, it becomes hard to see the evil as anything but the privation of goodness.

TRANSCENDENTAL GOODNESS

About twenty years ago, I attended a talk by the brilliant and saintly Stratford Caldecott (1953–2014). The talk was on G.K. Chesterton's idea that sometimes we need to see things upside down or backward in order to see them as they are. Chesterton's

8. Tolkien, *Lord of the Rings* 6.1, 914.
9. MacDonald, *Phantastes*, 56.

conviction was that everything is interesting and good, but the day-to-day business of life prevents most of us from recognizing this. Caldecott said something about seeing "a halo around every flower," a line of Chesterton's written in praise of George Mac-Donald. But Caldecott applied the praise to Chesterton himself.

I remember being intensely attracted to this way of seeing the world. But I was also troubled. I liked flowers. I loved trees and mountains. But it seemed to me that my experience of the things around me was impoverished relative to Chesterton's, or Mac-Donald's, or even Caldecott's. After the talk, the audience had some time to ask questions. In my eagerness, I forgot academic etiquette and asked a question better suited for spiritual direction than for literary society: "How do we come to see a halo around every flower?"

Now, I admire Caldecott very much. I have read several of his books and his talk that night was deeply inspiring. But I do not like the answer he gave me. The gist of his answer is that Chesterton was a genius, and his superior intellectual or artistic or prophetic powers made possible his mystical perspective on the world.

Part of the reason I do not like this answer is that I knew then and know better now that if genius is required to see the world shot through with goodness, there is no hope for me. But the more important reason I don't like his answer is that I now believe it to be false.

I believe it to be false because I have begun to see the world in the way Caldecott said Chesterton saw it. It hasn't been easy, and I have a long way to go. But it's happening. Here is how it is happening. First, I *want* to see the world this way. Or, better, I want to be in a world that really is shot through with good-ness. Of course, I don't want to have a perspective on the world that is false, and so, if goodness isn't out there in the world to be perceived, I don't want to perceive the world that way. I want the world to be that way, and I want to see it as it is. The persistence of this desire has shaped my vision, making it easier to discern the haloes. Second, in the years since Caldecott's talk, I have immersed myself in the classical and Christian tradition of philosophers and saints—arguably best exemplified by Aristotle and Aquinas, respectively—who have believed the world to be this way and who have explained their reasons, and I find their reasons good.

Consider, first, that everything that exists has a nature. There is no such thing as a bare *thing*; instead, there are oak trees and stars and people and water and so on. To be sure, we might *know* so little about a thing that we can do little more than identify it as a thing, as we do in the dark or when viewing something from a great distance—*what's that thing over there?* But despite our occasional ignorance, we know that, properly perceived, to see a thing is to see it as some *kind* of thing.

Second, for something to have a nature is for it to have some distinctive features and characteristic activities. Suppose you have some shiny yellow piece of metal and you are wondering whether it is gold or pyrite. Gold is smooth and easy to scratch; pyrite is crystalline and scratch-resistant. These characteristics help us to identify something as gold and not pyrite precisely because one set of characteristics is distinctive of gold and the other of pyrite.

I have already confessed that I haven't been to medical school, but I surmise that medical students learn about human health and sickness and disease and injury by studying a few examples: pictures in textbooks, cadavers in the lab. The presumption is that through the few examples the student gains expertise about human health and unhealth *in general* and not just the health and unhealth of the few examples. Of course, in medical practice, the future doctors will come up against cases that medical school has not fully prepared them for. The unusual or rare cases attest both to the incompleteness of medical knowledge and the great diversity among individual humans. But in the diversity, there is profound unity, and this unity undergirds the study and practice of medicine. More or less the same things can be said, *mutatis mutandis*, of the behavioral sciences. All humans share in the one human nature, so in getting to know the distinctive features and characteristic activities of human nature as such, we learn something important (though of course incomplete) about every individual human.

Third, a thing's nature serves as a sort of standard or measure against which the thing itself may be evaluated. We have good reason to think something is wrong with a person whose temperature is 104 degrees because the normal or ideal human temperature is about 98.6 degrees. If the oak tree's leaves are whitish or look rusty, we know something is wrong with the tree, and the arborist's efforts to help the tree are precisely efforts to do for the tree what it needs to align more closely with the ideal fixed by its nature.

To be sure, there are some kinds of things that don't seem to be susceptible of departing from the norms set by their natures—short of being simply destroyed. It makes little sense, for example, to speak of a defective piece of gold. It may be smaller than we'd like or require great labor to remove its impurities. But the gold as gold cannot be bad gold. Likewise, an electron can't be a defective electron. But while it is an intensely interesting fact about the world that there are things that cannot fail to express their natures fully, this is not wholly relevant.

Fourth, meeting or failing to meet the standard set by a thing's nature is the grounds for our judgments that things are good or bad. I do not mean here good or bad *for us*, or good or bad relative to our preferences or uses of things. The sort of conditions and diet that make for cheap rotisserie chickens at Costco may well be bad for chickens as such. Instead, I mean good and bad *simpliciter*, the way we might speak of a "good specimen" as the sort of thing that exemplifies its nature in a strikingly full way. Similarly, when we judge a thing to be doing *well* (literally, goodly) or *poorly* (badly), the judgment implies a comparison of the thing to its nature.

Fifth, the concepts of perfection and goodness are closely linked precisely because of the way in which being good is a matter of measuring up to one's nature. To be perfect is to lack nothing. To be perfect relative to a nature is to lack nothing belonging to that nature. Anything shy of perfection is by definition imperfect. But a thing might be imperfect in this technical sense and still be very good. A magnificent lion with one missing molar is an imperfect but excellent lion. There is some degree of imperfection below which it begins to make sense to call a thing bad, or doing badly. But we might have several descending degrees of imperfection before we reach a specimen it would make sense to call bad. And remember, evil and badness are just privations of goodness. It follows then, oddly enough, that even our magnificent lion with a missing tooth is a little bit bad. So if the perfect thing of a given nature is the best a thing with that nature can be, and many imperfect specimens of that nature are still good, even very good—despite the fact that they have privations of goodness—it makes sense to infer that even what counts as a bad specimen nevertheless has some measure of goodness. The really bad lion—gaunt, antisocial, malicious, like Scar—is still good, just insofar as he is a lion.

But from all this it follows that *everything is good*. Short of being annihilated, there is no way for a thing completely to abandon goodness, even if it is very bad. If it still exists, it still bears some degree of the perfection of its nature. Remember, pure evil literally does not exist. As long as you live, however wretched, you are still good. The same goes for everything else we encounter in this world of woe and decay: everything is good, just not as good as it could or should be. The tradition, perhaps first through Philip the Chancellor (1160–1236),[10] would come to call goodness a *transcendental property of being*, not in the sense that goodness is beyond being but because goodness transcends—crosses over, pervades—every being, just insofar as it exists.

THE CONSOLATION OF CONVERTIBILITY

One of the ways in which Boethius's philosophical outlook is more attractive than the Stoics' is his accommodation of the perception of goodness all around us, not only in *us*, in a morally upright life, but *out there*, in ordinary things.

Everything that is not Moral Worth itself, says Cicero's Marcus Cato, is a thing that is indifferent. The best he could say about some of these indifferent things is that they were more preferable than others.[11] But this is not good enough.

If you are staying at the Vermilion Resort in the Sierra Nevada Mountains in California, about three hours' drive east of Fresno, the fastest way to reach the John Muir Trail is by ferry. One of the hardy mountain men or women who staff the resort—which is actually little more than a campground with a store and a café and a few coin-operated showers—will cruise you across Edison Lake in a fishing boat to a shore close to the meeting of several trails. From there you can take the John Muir Trail north to Yosemite, or south to Mt. Whitney, or take any number of lesser trails to just about anywhere in the Sierras, if you've packed enough food in your pack or made arrangements to pick up food at distant mountain towns or other "resorts" like Vermilion.

One of the times I was ferried across Edison, I was with my brother and my two best friends. I was also with Boethius. I was

10. Aertsen, *Medieval Philosophy as Transcendental Thought*, 109–34.
11. Cicero, *De finibus* 3.15.

in college and had caught the philosophical bug my freshman year and was eager to learn more. So I brought a Penguin Classics copy of the *Consolation* with me to read by the fire and in the tent on our backpacking trip. Some of my best boyhood memories are simply being on a trail, looking ahead, seeing the lines of the path converge in the distance or disappear round a bend or over a hill. This particular trip was modest, as Sierras backpacking goes, but still sublime: we hiked about twelve miles to Silver Pass, dropped down to tiny Chief Lake, camped, spent the next day wandering around meadows and following streams to even tinier lakes, and hiked back to the ferry landing the third day, arriving at Vermilion in time to drive halfway down the mountain to meet my parents, who were camping at Dinkey Creek.

Wordsworth or Emerson or Thoreau or Muir himself are more obvious reading for a wilderness retreat—Muir especially if the retreat is in California. But it seems to me that Boethius is simply deeper and more important than these late admirers of the beauty of the natural world. There is nothing nostalgic or wistful about Lady Philosophy's cool syllogisms in support of the theses that all things are good and all things seek the good. She lays these out as matter-of-factly as a park ranger would instruct you about the geology and flora and fauna of the Sierra range. But for that very reason, I could begin to see the mountains and trees, meadows and wildflowers, streams and lakes and little glaciers as good in themselves, apart from their utility to me or even my preferences. They were just, good. Available for me to admire but not dependent on my perception for their value.

The convertibility of being and goodness—all beings are good, all good things are beings—is a consolation. We cannot help but perceive goodness as we move through the world. Modern philosophers drunk on physics can find no room for goodness in a world that is supposed to be real only to the extent it can be mathematically idealized. One Oxford philosopher from the second half of the twentieth century denied the reality of goodness on the grounds that in a world where physics must have the final word, objective value is "queer,"[12] in the old sense of "queer": odd, unfitting, unwelcome, like a bad smell emanating from the refrigerator. But normal people can smell the mountain air, or the scent of roses, of pipe tobacco and sawdust, spearmint and freshly mown grass, and know that there's nothing the least queer about the commonsense conviction that our perception of goodness is perception of things as they are. The convertibility of being and goodness is the philosophical insight that explains and defends this conviction.

But can it defend the conviction against reasonable objections? When I say that all things are good, am I telling you that mosquitoes are good? Am I telling you the COVID-19 virus is good? The pancreatic cancer that killed my grandpa and one of my dearest teachers: is that good? A nuclear weapon: good? Yes.

Or rather, yes and no. (What, did you think I was crazy?) Consider the mosquito. Obviously, they're bad for us. But there is a mosquito nature that the bajillions of mosquitoes more or less successfully live up to. A mosquito might be bad for us, but it is still good, even if its maximal degree of goodness is still pretty low. The same can be said for a virus: It's a thing in its own right with its own nature; why deny it its small share of goodness just because it is bad for us? As for cancer, it is one of the ways in which we ourselves go bad—not in the insensitive sense that cancer is our fault, for smoking or whatever—but in the literal sense that our own bodies produce the cancer that kills us. And a nuclear weapon is just a twisted way, in pursuit of twisted ends, to make use of the great energy-producing potential of certain isotopes of uranium and plutonium: an energy that can be harnessed to power cities just as well as it can be harnessed to destroy them.

12. Mackie, *Ethics*, 38–41.

The overwhelming majority of the universe is deathly inhospitable for us. The stars are far more dangerous than mosquitoes, but we do not consider them our enemies. They are far enough away not to bother us, so we are less distracted from seeing them as they are. Our sun is close enough to make life possible, and we are grateful, despite the fact that it is also close enough to cause sunburn and skin cancer. To be perfectly honest, the fact of mosquitoes doesn't bother me at all; I just don't want them to be in my backyard or in my campsite. But neither would I want the sun in my backyard or my campsite, as close to me as the mosquitoes too often are. I'd welcome a mosquito bite, even malarial, over instantaneous incineration any day.

What these superficially frivolous thoughts suggest is that it is not the *inventory* of things in the world that is problematic for the thesis that all things are good but their *arrangement*. Why should all these good things be so ruthlessly at odds with each other? Perhaps you track the arguments, and the sentiment, leading to the conclusion that all things are good, only to have your hopes dashed by the thought that the convertibility of being and goodness doesn't mean very much if it means the total order of the universe is bad. Closer to home, it might be comforting on certain occasions to consider that all people are good people, however deficient they are in goodness. But what gives, that the wicked (the very little good) should be permitted to inflict enormous injustice on the really good, or that the good should suffer at all, being good, and the bad should prosper at all, being bad? It is these very worries that prompt Boethius—himself a good man unjustly sentenced to die—to raise an anguished objection to Lady Philosophy's lesson.

8

The Greatest
Question of All

A DIFFERENT SORT OF EVIL

It is time again to think about what sort of consolation philosophy really can offer. Lady Philosophy has her fair share of the gruffness that is common (but not ubiquitous) among philosophers. But she also has qualities not so common: pastoral sensitivity, an understanding of how rhetoric and dialectic can play together in pursuit of the truth, and a poetic mind. But hers is not the consolation of poetry or rhetoric or prophecy or counsel. It is the consolation of *philosophy*. What is distinctive about this consolation? What, for all that, makes her conspicuous among philosophers, makes her consolation philosophical?

The correct answer cannot help but be boring. It is that she offers arguments for her conclusions. And when Boethius balks, her last recourse is simply to remind him that here is where the arguments have led. When the passions panic (C 4.1p), when the social instinct yearns to side with the majority opinion (C 4.76p), Lady Philosophy is there to remind him that however surprising their conclusions, they are built upon the rock of reason. If the conclusions are to be rejected, the only rational thing to do is to retrace their route and identify, if possible, the places they placed a wrong foot.

This is philosophy's only comfort in the end. It is not cool, it is not esoteric, it is not sophisticated. It does not have the allure either of antiquity or novelty. It does not dwell in hip cafés or beautiful libraries. It comes to those whose minds are empty enough to receive it, and it whispers, *do not be afraid to follow the arguments, wherever they lead.*

The question why, as a Christian, Boethius would in his darkest hour compose a book of philosophy's consolation, rather than Scripture's or theology's, has animated readers of Boethius for over a thousand years.[1] For now, it is enough to note this fact of religious life: religion bids us to believe wonderful things that are not obvious on their face. Should it really be a cause of scandal, or even wonder, that sometimes we want to examine the grounds of our beliefs? I mean, really, does anyone suppose it is a religious requirement to plug one's ears and shut one's eyes every time a potential objection comes our way? That sort of religion is merely servile and ideological, completely alien to Christianity and therefore to Boethius.

Imagine an artist or poet or novelist in Boethius's plight. Imagine an engineer or a carpenter or a mechanic. Philosophy is universal—everyone is already a philosopher before they set foot in Philosophy 101, I tell my students—but it stands to reason that in the prison of doubt and despair a different figure might figure more prominently in the consolation of the artist or mechanic than in the philosopher's. Boethius was a philosopher. Whatever additional consolation he may or may not have had, it makes sense that philosophy would be his consolation. And again, the only distinctively philosophical consolation philosophy can offer is to follow the arguments wherever they lead.

This preface is necessary to what follows because the conclusions Lady Philosophy and Boethius reach together are hard to

1. Shanzer, "Interpreting the *Consolation*," in *The Cambridge Companion to Boethius*, ed. Marenbon, 240.

accept. Boethius raises hard questions about the problem of evil that are not easily answerable with the resources so far set forth. He concedes the privation theory of evil, and he concedes the convertibility of being and goodness. But he's not yet convinced that these happy theses are enough to secure a rational foundation for belief, or hope, in God as the Good and in God as the providential sovereign of the universe.

The mere fact of badness no longer bothers Boethius. Augustine's final obstacle to embracing the Christian religion was the fact of evil.[2] There is genuine incompatibility between the claims that evil is a thing, and that God creates everything, and that God is perfectly good and so cannot make evil things. Augustine found his peace in part by embracing the privation theory of evil: everything is good, God made everything, and evil is not a thing in its own right but merely the privation of goodness. So far, the logic checks out.

Boethius raises an adjacent but somewhat different concern: even if we grant the convertibility of being and goodness, and the privation theory of evil, there still remains the problem of why the universe seems to be ordered in such a way that some who are good suffer and some who are wicked prosper (C 4.1p). If God who is the Good exercises providence over all things, and if God can do nothing contrary to his nature, we would expect that the good would always and everywhere prosper and the wicked would always and everywhere be thwarted. Evidently, this is not true (C 4.4p). So, something is wrong either with our notion of God or our assessment of the relative prosperity of the wicked and suffering of the good.

Lady Philosophy insists, then argues: the problem is not with our notion of God.

---

2. Augustine, *Confessions* 7.3(4).

THE GREATEST QUESTION OF ALL

It might not seem presumptuous to suppose that if a perfectly good God were to make a world with beings like us who can choose to do evil, he would exercise his providence in such a way that anyone inclined to do evil would be prevented from acting on their inclinations. Suppose a man raises a stick, intent to beat his dog. In our hypothetical world, God would prevent him from striking, the dog would be spared from harm, and the man would be spared from wrongdoing.

Sounds all right, at first. But then, shouldn't God have prevented him from raising the stick at all? Had he done so, the dog would have been spared the distress of fear. For that matter, shouldn't God have prevented him from forming the intention to beat his dog? From the flash of anger that led to the intention? After all, bad thoughts and feelings are still bad, even if less bad than bad actions. There's no reason to suppose God couldn't act at the level of the man's brain chemistry or sensory organs to prevent whatever perceptions or passions prompt his bad thoughts and feelings.[3] But now we're approaching a rather somber thought: to prevent evil, God might have simply prevented the man from existing at all. Turns out, God has very good reasons for making sure he never came into existence. Yet there he is. Despite his propensity to become irrationally violent to his dog when the dog chews his favorite slippers, God wanted him to exist. Similar things, of course, can be said of you and me.

So it is after all presumptuous to suppose that a perfectly good God would prevent all evil. Still, you might think there's a better version of this sort of complaint against God's providence. Wouldn't a perfectly good God ensure that the wicked pay for their wickedness? At the very least, the wicked should not be permitted to enjoy whatever they hope to gain by their wickedness. But it appears they often do. Moreover, the good guys should

3. Lewis, *Problem of Pain*, 24–25.

always win, should be rewarded for their goodness. But it appears that they do not and often are not. So, then, it is not the fact of wickedness that gives the lie to God's good providence but the fact that it goes unpunished and the good goes unrewarded.

But here, too, there is hasty presumption. Suppose we grant, as built into the notion of good providence, that *eventually* the wicked and the good will get what they truly deserve, that everyone will be fairly judged, *in the end*. Then the objection described in the preceding paragraph would go something like this: If God really exists and really is good and providential, he would not wait so long to restore justice. The wicked would be punished much sooner than the end of the world.

But how much sooner? What would quell the complaint? Should every bad deed be punished before the end of the evildoer's earthly life? Within a year of the bad deed? A day, an hour, a few seconds? Any timeframe we specify is more or less arbitrary. You might say, *as soon as possible*. So, God cannot wait so long as one second, since it is possible for him to do justice upon the evildoers a split-second sooner. Imagine our would-be dog-hitter: God, respecting his freedom, does not intervene to prevent him from striking his dog. But very shortly after striking the dog, God gives him the sensation of being struck with a stick and relieves the dog's pain. Surely, this would be one way for God to rectify the injustice of the dog-beating. If God acts too soon, the dog has no pain of which to be relieved. Grant there is a smallest-possible duration in which pain can be felt. Call it half a second. Then you might think that a perfectly good God would relieve the dog's pain no longer than half a second after the pain begins. Now, God is also supposed to give the man the pain that is due him for beating his dog. But for a punishment to be just, it must be proportionate to the crime. So God gives the man half a second of pain for punishment. What started as a call for immediate divine action for justice for the dog has become, by the objector's demands, petty cosmic bookkeeping. But God has better things to do.

These reflections go a long way to show that we are not very well positioned to make judgments about how the world would be if it really were governed by a perfectly good God. What starts as fairly intuitive points—If there were a God, he would prevent evil! If there were a God, he would not delay justice!—lead to conceptual quagmires: Can we really make a judgment that a world without you in it is better than a world in which you do some bad things? Can we really judge that justice requires the cancelling out of every evil action the soonest possible moment after it occurs? It appears we cannot.

Since we cannot, we should not weigh very heavily our intuitions about how the world could be better as evidence against the existence or goodness or providence of God.

But Boethius offers a better sort of objection that captures, I think, something of the flavor of the objections refuted here. Boethius does not seem especially concerned about the mere fact of wrongdoing, nor is he especially concerned about the speed of divine justice. Instead, what distresses him more than anything else is the apparent *randomness* of the worldwide distribution of affliction and blessing. "You see, I would wonder less if I thought that everything was mixed up through random chance, but the belief that God governs everything increases my amazement. One who often gives blessings to the good and harsh things to the bad, and then on the other hand offers difficulties to good men and fulfills the hopes of evil men—how would his actions differ from random chance, unless some explanation is found?" (C 4.5p, 129).

Lady Philosophy's sensible if insensitive reply is simply that the order of divine providence is not random at all but that Boethius is ignorant of its organizational scheme. "Just because you don't know the reasons for such arrangements, you shouldn't doubt that everything is done rightly, since a good ruler governs the world" (C 4.5p, 130). The man who does not even know the reason why the stars are constellated as they are—"the laws of heaven will stun his mind!" (C 4.5m, 130).

Fair enough, Boethius replies. But you, Lady Philosophy, are in the business of reasons and knowledge. "I beg you to tell me fully the reasons you find for this marvel, since it disturbs me greatly" (C 4.6p, 131).

To which she replies, "You're asking me to deal with the greatest question of all" (C 4.6p, 131).

THE ASTONISHING REPLY

In George MacDonald's fairy tale *Lilith*, the protagonist, Mr. Vane, inexplicably finds himself in the land of the dead. His guide is a wise Raven, who we later learn is Adam himself—as in *Adam and Eve*. Raven offers him some advice: "'In this world never trust a person who has once deceived you. Above all, never do anything such a one may ask you to do.' 'I will try to remember,' I answered; '—but I may forget!' 'Then some evil that is good for you will follow.' 'And if I remember?' 'Some evil that is not good for you, will not follow.'"[4] At worst, then, no matter what Mr. Vane does, he faces the prospect of *no final harm*. A failure to heed Raven's advice will result in an evil that is good for him, while following the advice will prevent an evil that is bad for him. It is only a minor spoiler to say that Vane does not heed Raven's advice, and both he and some people he loves suffer as a result of that failure. But it is, ultimately, good for him, and them. Had he heeded the advice, that suffering would not have followed and (so it is implied) the specific goods born of that specific suffering would not have followed, but some other goods would have.

4. MacDonald, *Lilith*, 135.

Which goods are better: the ones due to following the advice or ignoring it? We are never told.

This is mysterious, but it is not paradoxical. Imagine a range of options of things you might do right now. Whichever you pick, certain possibilities will be realized that would not have been realized had you picked a different option. The good, or the evil, that will come as a result of any of the options cannot be fully foreseen at the moment of choice. You are completely in the dark about the vast, vast majority of the total consequences that follow from any possible action you might or might not perform—after all, whatever you do right now initiates a series of events that extends throughout the future history of the world. Thank God that the moral evaluation of your actions does not depend on the total number of consequences, nor even fully depends on the relatively small number of foreseen consequences that follow from any of your actions!

To inhabit a providential world is to inhabit a world in which, for any action whatever, the whole series of events following from that action terminates in something good. God lets his creatures do their things but ensures that all that they do results in something good. That is the hope of providence: God will ensure that nothing in the end has been done wholly in vain or accomplishes finally evil ends.

Of course, we ourselves are in no position to tease out all the ramifications of every possible action. We literally cannot imagine all things working out for the good. "Even the very wise cannot see all ends," says Gandalf, comforting Frodo.[5] That soul most ardently abandoned to divine providence may nevertheless be almost totally agnostic about how exactly any particular event fits into the divine plan. To believe in divine providence has nothing to do with fortune-telling, except at the most general level of description: yes, I know the future, *and it is good*.

5. Tolkien, *Lord of the Rings* 1.2, 59.

Sometimes we are graced with hindsight, through which we can look back on some trial or trauma and see the good that has come *through*, and not just *despite*, it. Tolkien called the good ending wrought out of calamity *eucatastrophe*, the "good catastrophe."[6] In addition to gifts of hindsight, stories can also help us remain hopeful that the good will win out, in the end. In a eucatastrophic story like *Lord of the Rings* or C.S. Lewis's *Last Battle*, we experience the grimness but then win through to the good ending, seeing how the good comes out of the bad. In the story of your own life, you cannot yet see the finale, but good stories can train you to expect it will be finally good.

Belief that the direction of the universe aims at goodness fosters a certain way of seeing things—again, not fortune-telling, but an openness to searching for the good in things. A late former colleague of mine died too young of cancer. He did not want to die. But he spoke of the *gift* of cancer: it helped him appreciate things more deeply. This attitude, which seems to me saintly, can sit side by side with a wish the cancer would go away and leave him in peace to live out a full natural lifespan.

It really can be rational simultaneously to affirm cancer as a gift and to wish it would go away. You might *have no idea* whether it is overall better, in the grand scheme of things, to die of cancer at fifty or to recover and enjoy good health until old age, but remain *firmly committed* to the belief that good will come of it, no matter what.

In the sublimest and most difficult image of the whole *Consolation*, Lady Philosophy imagines God as the still center, or axis, of turning concentric circles. ("At the still point, there the dance is."[7]) This image is the foil to Fortune's wheel. I am inclined to think it is exactly the same wheel, now presented—after Boethius's long therapy—as it really is. The further out from the center

6. Tolkien, "On Fairy-stories," in *Tales from the Perilous Realm*, 384.
7. Eliot, "Burnt Norton" 2, *Four Quartets*, 15.

you go, the harder it is to discern the connection between the motion of those outer circles and their divine center. We can recognize that they are just as causally connected to their axis as the inner circles, but it is harder to see that connection. (Fortune's turnings, too, are ineffable.) Just so, everything that radiates from God's mind is according to a good plan, but the more remote effects of that radiation are harder to recognize as part of the plan. Back when Lady Philosophy deployed the medicine of rhetoric, those remote parts of the plan were said to be subject to fortune. But "fortune" connotes randomness or chance, and there is no room for chance in a providentially ordered world (C 5.1p). Now that providence has been established, Lady Philosophy tells us that the power that governs these remote effects is not fortune but fate. Fate is that part of the order of providence whose connection to providence we cannot discern but can trust is there.

We are creatures of the peripheries, invited to come closer to the center. We have the capacity, not only in thought but through the pursuit of virtue, to "seek the center of things" (C 4.6p, 134). In the whirl, we can hear the still small voice and choose to follow. In thought, we seek the center by *contemplating* the origin of all things: that it is good and wise and cannot create anything evil by nature. In the pursuit of virtue, we seek the center by *becoming* the sort of people who are godlike: good and wise and eager to bring about, or sub-create,[8] in our sphere of action, things that are good, however imperfect.

Freedom, says Lady Philosophy, belongs most completely to the virtuous. The vicious are slaves to their vices and make themselves incapable of achieving the good they seek by nature (C 5.2p). The virtuous, by contrast, to the extent they are virtuous and growing in virtue, are godlike and growing in divinity (C 3.10p). There is here a deep connection between freedom and motion toward the still center. The more closely you identify with

---

8. Tolkien, "On Fairy-stories," in *Tales from the Perilous Realm*, 361–62.

the center, the less you will interpret and feel unpleasant fate as a frustration of your deepest aims. By contrast, if all your hope for happiness lies in the outer circles, you are bound to feel unfree precisely because you have so little control over what happens.

We are all familiar, at least vaguely, with the concept of "centering" in various wellness movements. It's a very general concept that covers a wide variety of practices the purposes of which are to restore focus and tranquility. Some may be familiar with the practice of "centering prayer," popular in some Catholic circles, controversial in others, initiated by Thomas Merton, who wrote about contemplative prayer as a means to "find one's deepest center, awakening the profound depths of our being in the presence of God."[9] There is, perhaps, a danger that the effort to practice centering prayer achieves nothing more than self-centered prayer. But the centering we should truly seek is that by which we may find the deepest center of all, God himself who is our happiness and in union with whom we find our true selves.

"We have come, last and best, / From the wide zone through dizzying circles hurled, / To that still centre where the spinning world / Sleeps on its axis, to the heart of rest."[10]

ALWAYS GOOD

We cannot know, in any detail, the divine plan that permits the good to suffer and the wicked to prosper. What is all plan appears random to us. "All that is made seems random to the darkened mind, because there are more plans than it looked for. . . . There seems no plan because it is all plan."[11] Whether this is comforting or not depends, in part, on one's relationship to the center. I think it also depends on one's answer to certain questions about

9. Merton, *Contemplative Prayer*, 34.
10. Sayers, *Gaudy Night*, 243.
11. Lewis, *Perelandra*, in *The Space Trilogy*, 186.

freedom in a planned world, which we will be forced to confront in the following chapter.

But there is a little more Lady Philosophy has to tell Boethius by way of justifying the ways of God to man. Lady Philosophy implies that it really would be unjust of God to permit the wicked, by their wickedness, *truly* to prosper. And it would be unjust of God to permit the good, for their goodness, *truly* to suffer. "The good are always powerful and the wicked always abject and helpless." "Vices are never without punishment or virtues without reward." "Happiness always falls to good men and misfortune to evil ones" (C 4.1p, 110).

There is nothing blithe about Lady Philosophy's words, hard as they may be for us to accept. They are well-grounded in philosophical tradition. As Marenbon and others have noted, Lady Philosophy here channels Plato, whose Socrates says in *Gorgias* that the "admirable and good" person is always happy and the "unjust and wicked" person is always miserable, no matter what.[12] And implicit in the Stoic notion that the morally upright life is the only unconditionally good thing[13] is the conviction that no man is made truly happy by vice and wickedness. "Vice," said Chrysippus, "is the essence of unhappiness."[14] Lady Philosophy's words are also well-grounded in what she and Boethius have already conceded in their dialectical back and forth.

Everyone seeks the Good. We can think of the whole of life as one big action: the activity of pursuing the Good is this one life action. To accomplish an action is to perform the action successfully, to achieve what the action aims at. "Human actions are accomplished through two means: will and power," Lady Philosophy tells us (C 4.2p, 112). No one really does anything on purpose without in some sense wanting, or willing, to do it. And

12. Plato, *Gorgias* 470e; Marenbon, *Boethius*, 115.

13. Cicero, *De finibus* 3.11.

14. Plutarch, *On Stoic Self-contradictions* 1042A, in Long and Sedley, *Hellenistic Philosophers* 63H, 1:396.

no one achieves what they will to achieve if they lack the power to achieve it. But we have already agreed that in the one big activity of life, we all will the same thing: the Good. So if anything fails to achieve the Good, it is through lack of power, not will. To lack power is to be weak and to have power is to be strong. So those who achieve the Good are strong and those who fail to achieve the Good are weak.

Lady Philosophy continues: everyone who achieves the Good is good, and only the good achieve the Good. Of course, these two claims are consistent. But there is an ambiguity here: Do they become good by achieving the Good, as the first claim suggests? Or do they achieve the Good because they are good, as the second claim suggests? Lady Philosophy clearly thinks the former: people become good by achieving the Good. We know this is what she thinks because she says of evil men that if they acquired what they wanted, *they couldn't be evil*: achieving the good would make them good!

Now, from the claims that everyone seeks the Good, and only those with power get what they want, and only the good achieve the Good, it follows that only the good are strong.

But it is worth observing, to keep us linked to common sense as we track Lady Philosophy's reasoning, that none of us is purely good or purely evil. Remember, goodness comes in degrees. In this sense, we really can describe someone as *both* good and bad: having some degree of goodness that is lower than the upper limit, or being very good in some respects but not so good in others. Is Lady Philosophy trying to say that only the *perfectly good* achieve the Good? That only the *purely good* are happy?

Yes, that is exactly what she is saying. But here is why that is not as crazy as it sounds. Happiness, like goodness, comes in degrees. Any degree of happiness less than the ideal implies some degree of unhappiness. We encounter the same basic thought in the privation theory of evil: anything less than perfect is at least a little bit *im*perfect, however excellent it is; so too, anyone less than perfectly happy is at least slightly *un*happy, however happy he is. We might also say, on Lady Philosophy's behalf, that achievement of the Good is, too, the sort of thing that comes in degrees. A very happy person might be said to have achieved the Good more closely or more fully than a very unhappy person.

But all of these degrees of things let us see the good sense in Lady Philosophy's startling conclusion. To the extent to which one has achieved the Good, to that extent one is good. And, since the human good is happiness, one is happy to the extent one is good. For the same reasons, to the extent one has not (or not yet) achieved the good, to that extent one is bad or imperfect. And to that extent, one is unhappy. Therefore, only the good are happy (happy to the extent they are good) and only the bad are unhappy (unhappy to the extent they are bad). Everyone desires happiness; only the good achieve happiness (to the extent they are good). Therefore, only the good are strong—strong to the extent they are good.

And only the bad are weak—weak to the extent they are bad. Lady Philosophy goes so far as to say that evil men don't exist. "I don't deny that evil men are evil, but I do deny that they exist in a real and essential way" (C 4.2p, 115). Remember, to be bad is to lack some goodness one ought to have, and the purely bad is the same as nonexistence.

But if the wicked are so weak they do not so much as exist (to the extent they are wicked), why are the wicked able to wreak havoc on this good world and especially on good and therefore innocent people? Whatever true power they have comes from whatever degree of goodness remains to them. Whatever is wicked about them is weak. Notice: God who is the Good cannot do evil. And there is nothing that God cannot do. So evil is nothing. Thus, to the extent men do evil, to that extent they do nothing.

BEYOND BELIEF?

This is genuinely difficult to take seriously, let alone to believe. But I do take it seriously, and I am on my way to believing it. So please hear me out. In this last section of this chapter, I will try to make all this seem a bit more plausible and attractive.

To say that some wicked action is nothing is not to say that it is an illusion. Remember, Lady Philosophy said the same thing about wicked men: they don't exist (C 4.3p). She means that what is wicked about them is precisely where there is a privation of goodness: the hole in the sweater, the blindness in the eyes. The same for actions: what is bad about the action is what is not there. A murder by stabbing, for example, combines, let's say, the physical strength and powerful anger of the murderer, the rigidity and sharpness of steel, the softness of human flesh, and brings about an unjust death. But all the positive things we list about the murder are good in themselves, or at the very least can be used for good—even anger has its place in the virtuous life. The wrongness of the murder consists in what the action lacks: love of one's neighbor and circumstances (say, self-defense) that justify killing this particular person.

The other thing to say about wicked actions is that they may be used by God in his providence to bring about goodness. What you intended for evil, God intended for good, Joseph tells his repentant brothers.[15]

Way back in chapter 4 we considered Lady Philosophy's distinction between felicity and beatitude (C 3.1p), where beatitude is the true happiness we seek and felicity is the happiness of a good mood or a good feeling. Being sad or in pain is incompatible with felicity but not at all incompatible with beatitude. By definition, pain and sadness are less pleasing than pleasure, but we all recognize one sense in which it is *good* to feel pain and sadness: if your friend is very sick, or your dog dies, or you are

---

15. See Genesis 50:20.

injured, it is good to be grieved or disappointed in the sense that these are appropriate responses to these events. Grief and disappointment are two forms beatitude takes when the happy person confronts loss of or harm to things held dear.

That much, at least, should be relatively uncontroversial. But Lady Philosophy insists on a second sense in which it is good to feel pain and sadness: by mysterious providence, every fortune that befalls a man is completely good. "Since all fortune, either pleasant or bitter, is given to reward or test the good or to punish or correct the bad, it is entirely good, since it is either just or useful" (C 4.7p, 141). Here, she doubles down: everything that happens is good *for us*. This includes, implicitly, the suffering inflicted on the good by the wicked.

No one's fate or fortune is intended entirely for his own benefit: providence does or lets happen to him what promotes the common good, not just his own good. For the good, the pleasant is a reward or respite and the bitter a trial or challenge to grow in virtue. Others, looking at the rewards of the good, may find the life of virtue more attractive and want to emulate it. The same, looking at the trials of the good nobly endured, may find solace in their own troubles. For the bad, the bitter is punishment and as for the pleasant, well, the virtuous can see that the sorts of things the wicked find pleasant, insofar as they are wicked, do not make for authentic happiness: the pleasure the wicked take in their wickedness is itself part of what makes the wicked life wretched. But pleasant twists of fate for the wicked can also be a mercy, for the wicked man and those around him: "If someone has such a headstrong and violent nature that poverty might drive him to crime—Providence offers a cure for his disease by providing him with money" (C 4.6p, 138).

Nothing in Lady Philosophy's consolation gives a formula for deciphering the precise form or degree of goodness God intends to bring about by any particular event. We may not be able to see the good in some or even many of the things that befall us. The point of Lady Philosophy's examples is instead to foster belief that even when things seem topsy-turvy—the good suffering, the wicked at ease—good things are afoot.

We must always remember that none of us is wholly good or wholly wicked. The wholly good is God alone, whereas to be *wholly* wicked would be not to exist at all. The line between good and evil cuts through the human heart, in Solzhenitsyn's famous line.[16] This means that when Lady Philosophy explains how the pleasant and bitter alike are good for the good and good for the wicked, she is talking about each of us individually: you yourself are, I myself am, the good *and* the wicked she is talking about. Whatever is bad in you, providence is sending things your way to get you into shape and to protect or warn others. Whatever is good in you, providence is sending things your way to comfort or bless you but also to challenge you. The human heart is complex, but it cannot confuse providence.

I take great comfort in this, as one of those people in the in-between. All the good in me I know, at my best moments, is not enough to ensure a life of temporal bliss. As for all the bad in me, at my best moments I wonder why judgment has not come more heavily on me.

You might object that I say this, so you surmise, as one who has not known the deepest depths of misery a human being is capable of suffering. But it's not me, it's Boethius the author putting all this in Lady Philosophy's mouth, writing as a prisoner unjustly condemned to die. Even Job persevered in hope. Viktor Frankl, no stranger to the suffering that, some think, is the only qualification to speak on the subject, said that the suffering of two individuals is always incommensurable: Which is worse, to have been in a concentration camp or in the Battle of Stalingrad?[17]

16. Solzhenitsyn, *Gulag Archipelago* 4.1, 615.
17. Frankl, *Yes to Life*, 98–101.

He could not say, because he knew there was no answer. There is wisdom here, and the root of compassion. You do not know exactly what it is like to feel what another feels. A physical trial that is overwhelming for others for you is bearable, let's say; but then a social upheaval that overwhelms you, others can manage without undue distress. We all suffer some degree of the privation of goodness, nor are our privations of exactly the same species: where you are lacking, others have abundance while you abound in what others lack. Let us be good to one other. And even when we are not good to one another, let us live in hope—ideally, hope *and belief*, but even hope alone has some consolation—that there is a power beyond the world ordering even our failures to the Good.

9

Freedom and Why It Matters

THE PHILOSOPHICAL PROBLEM

The denial that there is consciousness is probably "the silliest claim ever made."[1] But there is a rival. Some people deny that we have free will. The methods used to show the stupidity of the denial of consciousness work equally well to show the stupidity of the denial of free will. It is a datum of science that there are people. Without people, there could be no science and no philosophical reflection on science, even the most idiotic reflection on science. There are some people who cannot engage in anything we can recognize as scientific or philosophical thought: the very young, for example, or the severely cognitively impaired, or the comatose. But the very young are immature, and the cognitively impaired are impaired, and the comatose are comatose, and these are the explanations for the fact that, being persons, they nevertheless cannot engage in scientific or philosophical thought. And part of the nature of personhood is to be able to be aware of oneself and to control oneself. These features of personhood are evident in our experience. Right now, you are engaged in an activity that, should you complete it, is the activity of reading this sentence to its end. (Thank you!) At any moment that activity

1. Strawson, "The Consciousness Deniers."

might have been interrupted: maybe you decided to check the football scores, maybe the fire alarm went off. But also, maybe, you decided to stop reading. In reading this sentence, right now, you are perfectly aware of your ability to stop reading, should you choose. You are also perfectly aware of your ability to read this sentence.

Of course, people have made arguments to support the conclusion that we are not free after all. Some reason from a supposed feature of the world they think science compels us to adopt: our actions are physical events; physical events are causally determined by other, prior physical events; so, our actions are determined, not free. Others reason from theology: God knows everything that is going to happen because he has planned it all out beforehand. But if God is pulling the strings, then we are not free after all.

But whatever merit these sorts of arguments might have, it is not rational to be persuaded of their conclusions by their premises. This is because the truth of any of the premises is nowhere near as evident to us as is the truth that we are free. We cannot rationally deny our freedom; but we can rationally deny the truth of any of the premises in arguments for determinism. Therefore, confronted with an argument for determinism, even an argument we cannot refute, we ought to conclude that it is refutable, even if we can't see exactly what's wrong with it. Freedom is simply a given that any reasonable philosophical outlook must accommodate.

It is good to keep this in mind while reading this final chapter, as we consider the final philosophical problem Boethius and Lady Philosophy tackle together. Having understood and accepted Lady Philosophy's discourses on providence and fate, Boethius now wonders what place freedom has, or can have, "in this series of causes bound together." "Does the chain of Fate bind every movement of human souls?" (C 5.2p, 149).

On the surface, it seems she must say *yes*. She has already proclaimed that the course of fate, rooted in providence, "binds the actions and fortunes of men by an unbreakable chain of causes" (C 4.6p, 134), and this looks like as strong a metaphor for determinism as any. But of course, Lady Philosophy must make room for freedom. In the remainder of this chapter, we'll consider how she makes room for freedom, and why it matters.

THE PERSONAL PROBLEM

We all have our reasons not just for thinking we are free but for valuing freedom as highly as we do. Speaking anecdotally, most people hold their freedom dear because freedom is a necessary condition for moral responsibility. Without freedom, there can be no praise or blame. But these types of evaluations are baked into our self-understanding, personal relationships, legal system, and ethical norms so fundamentally as to make life without praise or blame unrecognizable as a life we can call our own. Confronted with a challenge to free will, the same Boethius who had once asked why God does not punish all bad deeds, now asks why God would punish at all if evil-doers do not act freely. "This would seem to be the greatest injustice of all . . . that wicked men be punished or good ones rewarded, since these men would [be] compelled by the fixed necessity of the future" (C 4.3p, 155).

But Boethius has an even deeper reason for valuing free will. Lady Philosophy, step by step, had rekindled Boethius's hope in God—not just a hope that there is a God who is good and wise but a hope that we can have some sort of ennobling and satisfying relationship with that God. Our pursuit of happiness, recall, is nothing more or less than our pursuit of union with God, *divinization* (C 3.10p). In this life, it is virtue but especially prayer and "divine grace" that unite us with God, even as we wait for a deeper union after death (C 4.3p, 156). But in a totally fatalistic world, prayer would have no point and our virtuous actions would not be our own. But "then what will there be that will let us connect with the highest Lord of all things and become united with Him?" (C 4.3p, 156). That divinization, which was the most wholesome medicine Lady Philosophy had to offer, now seems both out of reach and unattractive. Even if we could, why would we want to be united with a God who is the sole "Author of all things" and therefore the one from whom all "our faults proceed" (C 4.3p, 155)?

So, the knotty problem of free will and providence is personal, not merely philosophical. But before moving on to the solution, let us remember what's really at stake as we consider the problem. There can be no real doubt that we do in fact have free will. That is a given. Now, Boethius sees a potential conflict between that given and the conclusions so far reached about God's existence, goodness, and providence. If the probing of this potential conflict reveals a genuine inconsistency between our freedom and any of these theses about God, one or more of these theses needs to go. So what is really threatened here is not the freedom that is essential to our lives but the existence and nature of the God that makes our lives ultimately meaningful.

TWO KINDS OF FREEDOM

Causal determinism is one of the central doctrines of Stoicism. God and the world are one and the same (pantheism), and everything that exists is physical. There is nothing beyond the world and nothing spiritual. For any event whatsoever, including human actions, the causal history of the universe leading up to that event totally causes that event to occur. The present and future are therefore as fixed as the past: in the Stoic system, there is no room for random anomalies like Lucretian swerves, or divine interventions by God or the gods of the Greco-Roman pantheon, or unpredictable inputs from human free will.

But the Stoics recognized, if only implicitly, that we cannot live with this view of the universe. They therefore tried to salvage a notion of freedom. According to the salvaged notion, our freedom makes no causal contribution to the universe. Everything that happens to us and everything we do is totally determined. Nevertheless, they thought, we *do* have some control over our *attitude* about what happens. Hence the Stoic focus on cultivating the cardinal virtues, the virtues that equip us to endure bitter fortune with equanimity and pleasant fortune moderately. As Marcus Aurelius exhorted himself, "You are an old man, suffer this governing part of you no longer to be in bondage, no longer to be a puppet pulled by selfish impulse, no longer to be indignant with what is allotted in the present or to suspect what is allotted in the future."[2]

The wise emperor can't fully embrace the thought that destiny determines everything. He sees inside himself a power to accept or resist what destiny appoints even for his own body: powerful urges like the desire for sex might seem like the sort of thing we have no control over. But Marcus Aurelius sees otherwise.

The same insight is expressed in the famous image of the dog tied to a cart, attributable all the way back to Zeno, the first Stoic. "When a dog is tied to a cart, if it wants to follow it is pulled and follows, making its spontaneous act coincide with necessity, but if it does not want to follow, it will be compelled in any case. So it is with men too: even if they do not want to, they will be compelled in any case to follow what is destined."[3] So the more we learn to endure willingly whatever direction fate's wagon pulls us, the less miserable we'll be.

2. Marcus Aurelius, *Meditations* 2.2, trans. Farquharson, 10.
3. Hippolytus, *Refutation of all Heresies* 1.21, in Long and Sedley, *Hellenistic Philosophers* 62A, 1:386.

Let's call this sort of freedom the freedom of *reaction*. And call the sort of freedom Stoicism denies, the freedom of *action*. Stoics deny we have freedom of action, but they insist we have freedom of reaction. Our freedom of reaction is supposed to be the sort of thing of which we can have more and less. It increases as we grow in virtue and decreases as we become vicious. The virtuous are free insofar as their tranquility of mind does not depend on pleasant circumstances; and when subject to the powerful urges of the body, they do not compulsively obey.

The question is whether the Stoics can have it both ways: to hold on to determinism and deny the freedom of action, while preserving the freedom of reaction in the protected zone of the interior life.

The answer is that they cannot. One's acceptance of (or re-sistance to) the pull of the wagon is just as much a thing that happens as anything else. It is entirely arbitrary—at best—to sup-pose that within the physical boundaries of one's skull or body is a self-determining power exempt from the total series of causes that determine everything else. But I think it is worse than arbitrary. The distinction between inside and outside turns out to be rather hard to make when we are dealing with human action. Start with this image: the dog's resistance to the wagon is ultimately futile— the wagon will win. But an act of resistance may well include physically tugging against the wagon's pull. It does not matter that the winner of the tug-of-war is predetermined. The taut rope of the resister is a different kind of physical outcome than the slack rope of the accepter. The degree of tension on the rope in turn contributes to the total causal input that determines what comes next in the universe.

Likewise, if despite my great weakness for pizza, I follow the Stoic manuals and grow in temperance, I make myself able to resist the allure of the pizza. There it is on the table, in all its glory. As a virtuous man, I need not go for it. The old me, prior to my acquisition of temperance, would have been helpless to resist. But the problem is that my newly acquired inner freedom over my reaction to the pizza makes the world go differently than it would have if I had remained a slave to my tastebuds. After all, without temperance, all the pizza on the table—*out there*—is gone; with temperance, only one or two pieces are gone. Moreover, if we consider the total causal story that explains how I was able to grow in virtue, we must make reference to things *out there*: the Stoic manuals, the wise teachers, and so on. On the Stoic system, it would be inexplicable coincidence for there to be a perfect chronological syncing of my self-determination to improve myself by reaching for the Stoic manual with the causal determination of the circumstances that result in the book in my hand.

The conclusion, then, is that the freedom of reaction cannot stand independently of the freedom of action. They stand or fall together: so the Stoic or aspiring Stoic really ought to concede that one's reactions to circumstances are just as determined as everything else. The wisdom, justice, temperance, and fortitude of the Stoic master are not his to claim as his own: their development is just as determined as the weather.

Lady Philosophy recognizes that these two kinds of freedom stand or fall together. We do have the freedom of reaction the Stoics insisted we have; but we also have the freedom of action that they denied. Part of what it is to be a person is to have free will: "Rational natures could not exist if there were no freedom of the will" (C 5.2p, 149). "By its own power," a rational nature "determines what it should seek and what it should avoid" (C 5.2p, 149). This sort of freedom cannot be lost except by annihilation of the person who has it.

Nevertheless, there is an adjacent sense of freedom according to which it makes sense to describe someone as more or less free. The more virtuous, the more godlike, are "more free" than those who are "given over to vices and fall away from the possession of their reason" (C 5.2p, 150). These vicious people endure the "ultimate slavery," a slavery especially debased because "they're made captive by their own freedom" (C 5.2p, 150). But however free or ensnared we are with respect to this sort of freedom, we can never lose that congenital freedom that is one of the essential marks of the sort of agents we are. Our distinctively personal way of contributing to the total causal order of the world is by our free choices.

And it is just this distinctively personal contribution to the causal order that seems to be in tension with the order of providence. It is time to consider Lady Philosophy's attempt to resolve the tension.

THE SOLUTION

Suppose my wife asks me to stop at the grocery store to get what we need for dinner. "Sure thing," I say, "What are we having?" "I didn't have a plan. You pick." Offered the choice, I contemplate a range of relevant considerations: my own preferences, my wife's, the kids', what we've already had for dinner this week, and so on. After some deliberation, I decide to make chicken soup. So commences a long series of actions culminating in the eating of the soup: purchasing ingredients, taking them home, making the soup out of those ingredients, setting the table, dishing up, saying grace, and digging into the soup. The world takes a chicken soup turn partially as a result of my choice to make chicken soup—or so it seems. And the world would not have taken a chicken soup turn without my choice—or so it seems. What we need is an account of providence that lets us affirm that things are as they seem.

It was the problem of free will and *providence* that launched Boethius's anguished questions. But as he unfolds his concerns, he focuses explicitly on what seems at first to be a different problem:

the problem of free will and *foreknowledge* (C 5.3p). And Lady Philosophy explicitly formulates a solution only to the problem of foreknowledge, not of providence (C 5.4p).

Here is a simple way to see the difference between the two problems. Foreknowledge, as the word suggests, is *knowledge* of a thing before it happens. But providence suggests making a plan and ensuring the plan works out. Providence therefore connotes God's own causal contribution to the universe, whereas divine foreknowledge connotes merely God's knowledge of the future of the universe. The problems these pose seem different on the surface: a solution to the foreknowledge problem seeks a way to reconcile God's knowledge of what I do before I do it, with my freedom to bring it about; while a solution to the providence problem seeks a way to reconcile God's planning and execution of all things with my ability to act freely. One commentator—and one of the best, at that—complains that even if she succeeds in resolving the tension between freedom and foreknowledge, Lady Philosophy never addresses the problem of freedom and providence![4]

So, has Lady Philosophy just dodged one of Boethius's central questions, and if so, why? Is she coming to her wits' end, as the same commentator suggests?[5] I do think she is approaching her wits' end, but I don't think she is dodging the question. Once we understand what providence is, and what foreknowledge is—as Boethius the author understands these, anyway—we can see that a solution to the problem of freedom and foreknowledge works equally well as a solution to the problem of freedom and providence.

To see this, we must consider Lady Philosophy's most careful formulation of what providence really is. "The origin of all things, and all growth of beings with changing natures, and all things that

---

4. Marenbon, *Pagans and Philosophers*, 51–53.

5. Marenbon, *Pagans and Philosophers*, 53.

are moved in any way obtain their causes, their order, and their form from the stability of the Divine Mind. The Mind, settled in the citadel of its own simplicity, has determined many means for accomplishing its purposes. The means that is viewed in terms of the purity of Divine Intelligence itself is called Providence. When we speak of things that are set in motion and arranged, the means has been called Fate in the past" (C 4.6p, 132).

Here is the crucial takeaway: providence is here identified with something going on in God's mind. The passage is admittedly difficult, but the basic picture is this: prior to anything else existing, God knows the natures of all things, how they can come about, and how they can be arranged spatially and temporally. We can think of these natures as so many possible creatures, and we can think of different possible total arrangements of things as possible worlds. Knowing all these possible worlds, God purposes to make one of them. Insofar as God knows the world he purposes to make before he makes it, God has knowledge of everything that occurs in that world's past, present, and future. Providence, therefore, entails God's foreknowledge (and present knowledge, and past knowledge).

When God creates the world, it unfolds according to plan. But that plan includes "many means for accomplishing its purposes." Within the Divine Mind itself, in which the plan for the world takes shape, the only real power is the Divine Mind itself—nothing that exists only in the Divine Mind is truly active. Things *actually* act and move in accordance with their natures and in concert with other things only if they *actually exist*. Once God launches his plan by making the world, things operate according to their natures, just as God conceived them. "Fate" is the name given to the total system of the world of things acting according to their natures. The point here, however, is not that things are fated in the sense that God is forcing everything to happen. Instead, the point is that everything that exists has a nature and nothing can act in a way altogether contrary to its nature. If God deigns to make a thing, he deigns to make a thing that can do things.

But here's the upshot: among the actual things in nature are *people* and it is essential to people to have the power of free will. So, when we are told that God "has determined many means for accomplishing his purposes," we must infer that one of these means is the free actions of free people. The free actions of people are among the distinctively personal contributions people make to the world.

Providence, then—at least as Boethius understands it—has to do with God dreaming up worlds, purposing to make a world, and bringing the world about, in which creatures can exercise their natural powers. God moves creatures in the general sense that he is the Good at which all things aim. And of course, God can intervene more directly—causing miracles, let's say, or taking on the human form, as Christians say he did. But God's prerogative to intervene and his status as the Good at which all things aim are far, far away from a fatalistic world in which God makes everything happen.

So understood, a solution to the problem of foreknowledge suffices as a solution to the problem of providence. The real concern—and Lady Philosophy discerns that this is the heart of the issue—is that, if God has a grand plan for the world tucked away in his mind from all eternity, he already knows what I am going to do. And God cannot be wrong. You might say that God knows with certainty what I am going to do. And that, at first glance, compromises freedom. It is very easy to slide from God's certainty of my future action, to thinking that my future action is fated, to thinking that my future action is not something I really do by my own free will.

Not so fast, cautions Lady Philosophy. First, consider that if what God foreknows is a *free* action, then God knows it as freely done. If it really is a free action, then God cannot know it as unfree—he would be wrong, and God can't be wrong! So, when God foreknows your free actions he knows them as freely done. "His divine foreknowledge does not change the nature or integrity of things" (C 5.6p, 169).

Second, consider that in general, knowing something to be so does not make it so. If you observe a man making soup, you know he is making soup. But you are not making him make soup. That much is obvious. But then, "just as knowledge of things in the present conveys no necessity on them as they happen, so the foreknowledge of future things places no necessity on them to make them come about" (C 5.4p, 160). To avoid misunderstanding the point of the analogy, we need to keep in mind that the source of God's knowledge of creatures is not the same as ours. You know the man to be making soup by observing him. God knows the man to be making soup by knowing the contents of God's own mind. You are the reader, God is the author, so to speak. In these respects, God's knowledge is *not like* ours. But Boethius's analogy is limited. God's knowledge *is like* ours in this one respect: knowing, even God's knowing, is not the same as causing and does not imply causing.

Third, entertain the thought that God does not exist in time like you and I do. God, says Boethius, is eternal, and "eternity is total and perfect possession at one time of unlimited life" (C 5.6p, 167)—a divine attribute that follows from divine simplicity. Then, plausibly, God knows all at once the things that we index as past, present, and future. But then God's knowledge of the future would be like your knowledge of the man eating soup. The future would be just like the present as far as God's knowledge is concerned. But if we don't feel our freedom threatened by the thought that God knows what we are doing right now, we shouldn't feel it threatened by the thought that he knows what we will do tomorrow (C 5.4p).

THE END OF PHILOSOPHY

The relationship between foreknowledge and free will and the history of thinking about that relationship are deep and complex and quickly reach a level of philosophical technicality unsuitable for this book, which is not a book on foreknowledge but on the Boethian worldview written in sympathy with that worldview. It would take a book much longer than this to explore the whole conceptual and historical terrain of that relationship.

Boethius has done enough, so I judge, to preserve the coherence of human freedom and divine foreknowledge. He shows that there is nothing logically inconsistent between these. Foreknowledge, it turns out, is God's thorough knowledge of the details of the world he planned out before he created it. He does not know the world by observing it from the perch of eternity. Instead, he conceived a grand story full of things and people of diverse natures and temperaments, then willed that story into being. As soon as it was real, the plot began to unfold. Everything acts according to its nature: the merely natural act naturally, and the free act freely. This is the sort of world God chose to make. He didn't need to make a world with people in it; but he did. His providential plan makes room for the free actions of free people, and when he knows their actions, part of what he knows is that they are done freely.

All this is a great achievement of Lady Philosophy. It was no easy problem Boethius posed to her. And he posed it after countless hours of philosophical back and forth in which she had to assume the complementary but different roles of therapist and dialectician. She's put in a long day's work! And she was still up for the task. But she is coming up against her limit.

The consolation of philosophy is philosophical consolation, and that means offering arguments. In the service of arguments, Lady Philosophy also makes distinctions and defines concepts. She reaches her limits precisely when the arguments reach their limits. And here, in the face of the various and difficult issues surrounding evil and providence, foreknowledge and free will, she reaches her limits. These topics are susceptible to philosophical evaluation, but they are not susceptible to full analysis. Rate her achievement ever so high, Lady Philosophy's defense of freedom does not dispel the mystery of freedom and foreknowledge.

The relationship between freedom and foreknowledge was a *problem* as long as Boethius was worried about logical incompatibility. The threat of incompatibility (let us grant) has been neutralized. But clever arguments offered for the sake of preserving consistency are nowhere close to a full disclosure of everything there is to be known about the relationship of freedom and providence. There is still the *mystery* of that relationship. How did God conceive the idea of something other than himself? How did he make a thing other than himself, let alone a thing with freedom? How can there be a thing whose action depends on causes outside itself but, given all the causes it needs to act, is free to direct that causal input this way or that as it chooses? Little gods, indeed! How did God make such a thing?

Why, falling so far short of human perfection, and knowing everything I would freely do, would God make a world with me in it? I certainly don't deserve to have been made. I am grateful I'm here. But even considering merely human fiction, I can think of a few examples of people it would have been better to bring about: surely a world with Aragorn son of Arathorn in it would be better, all else being equal, than a world with me in it. But we cannot actually know this, because we can't know everything else that would be different about the world if we swap one person for another. Had my wife married Aragorn, she might have been happier, but then, they wouldn't have made the children she and I have made. Fanciful what-ifs are fun and wholesome, but we lack the imagination and wisdom to reverse engineer a better world.

What is the good of some *particular* suffering—a child's violent death, terminal cancer in a young mother, severe depression, or an unjust death sentence? Philosophy cannot disclose God's plans at this level of detail; she can only offer support for the general claim that God ensures that things work out for the good.

If God knows everything in an eternal present, does the temporal sequence in which we live our lives matter to him? Do the past, present, and future intermingle in God's mind? If so, could something I will experience in the future be a cause of something I experienced in the past? Or, if the tenses intermingle, is the past as fixed as we think it is?

I offer no answers to these questions, not only because I don't know the answers but because I want to draw attention to some small slice of the scope of questions unanswered and perhaps unanswerable by a philosophical argument for the compatibility of freedom and providence. For the restless inquiring soul, a cogent argument for their compatibility is minimally intellectually satisfying. It raises far more questions than it answers.

The best that philosophy can do, when it comes to divine things, is not nearly good enough. But it is still good. "Not in vain are hopes and prayers placed before God," Lady Philosophy says as she approaches her conclusion. She continues, and these are her last words, and the last words of the *Consolation of Philosophy*: "So let us shun vices and cultivate virtues, lifting our minds to proper hopes and offering humble prayers on high . . . since you live in front of a judge who sees all things" (C 5.6p, 173).

Epilogue

The Faith of Boethius

PREPARATION FOR DEATH

When it was time for him to die, the great Socrates did not mind. In fact, he was eager. He looked forward to death as a portal to a postmortem life of uninterruptible contemplation of divine things.[1] His death was not the victory his Athenian enemies sought against their philosophical gadfly. The cup of hemlock they made him drink was the means by which he achieved exactly what he most desired. For the true philosopher, there is consolation even in death.

One commentator, Joel Relihan, has suggested that death itself was the very consolation Lady Philosophy had meant to offer Boethius. All the words between them were words of preparation, meant to prepare him not just to welcome his death but take his own life, go out on his own terms.[2] On this reading, the "homeland" to which she intended to lead him (C 1.5p, 5.1p) is the homeland of the philosophers' heaven: eternal contemplation of divine things, in the company of Socrates.

The sages lack a consensus about the permissibility of suicide. Socrates was emphatic that it is always wrong to take one's own life.[3] But several Stoics thought suicide is permissible, at least

---

1. Plato, *Phaedo* 63b–e.
2. Relihan, *Prisoner's Philosophy*, 5.
3. Plato, *Phaedo* 61c–d.

under certain conditions.[4] Famously, the Stoic Cato the Younger (95–46 BC) took his own life, finding death preferable to life under Caesar's looming tyranny.[5] Seneca attempted to associate Stoic suicide with the death of Socrates: "Socrates was ennobled by the hemlock draught. Wrench from Cato's hand his sword, the vindicator of liberty, and you deprive him of the greatest share of his glory."[6]

But this association is unfair to Socrates. He was sentenced to death by the Athenian senate. The means they selected for his execution was hemlock. We might concede he had some choice in the matter: to drink the cup offered him or have it poured down his throat. One is obviously nobler than the other. But neither is suicide.

On the doubtful supposition that Lady Philosophy meant to prepare Boethius to kill himself, her therapeutic endeavor was a spectacular failure. After all, at page 1, Boethius was already eager to die (C 1.1m). And by the end, prompted by his persistent questions about evil and freedom, foreknowledge and providence, she is urging him to "shun vices and cultivate virtues," to lift his mind "to proper hopes," and to offer "humble prayers on high" (C 5.6p, 173). The question of suicide is nowhere to be found.

You know what else is nowhere to be found? Boethius himself. Lady Philosophy's final speech closes the *Consolation*, and we're left to speculate whether Boethius is there listening attentively, or has dropped to his knees in prayer, or has been carried off to the executioner. I prefer to think that Lady Philosophy and Boethius the *prisoner* have become one in the person of Boethius the *author*. With those final words, Boethius is exhorting himself, and us. He (and we) will die soon, but no earthly power can take away his (our) virtue or his (our) hope in God.

---

4. Sandbach, *The Stoics*, 52.

5. Drogula, *Cato the Younger*, 294.

6. Seneca, "Letter 13.14," in *Moral Letters to Lucilius*, trans. Gummere, 34.

Remember Meursault in *The Stranger*? He believed the universe to be "benignly indifferent" to the cares and hopes and sufferings of men. In this frame of mind, he expressed his one ultimate hope (which is no real hope): that at his execution, he would hear "howls of execration." Approaching his own execution, and believing the universe to be good and ordered by God who is the Good, the one ultimate hope of Boethius is divinization. One of these is better than the other. Choose wisely.

FAITH AND REASON

The *Consolation* has some similarity with ancient satirical writing,[7] so Relihan supposes that the *Consolation* is itself satirical: it shows up the inadequacy of philosophy for addressing the questions of deepest importance to us. In this way, says Relihan, *Consolation* is a deeply Christian book: it encourages the Christian reader to look to his faith and not to philosophy for consolation.[8]

The problem with this thesis is that it presupposes that faith and philosophy are antagonistic endeavors, that one either looks to philosophy for guidance or to faith, but cannot look to both.

But we have no reason to accept this dichotomy between faith and philosophy, and no reason to think Boethius accepted the dichotomy. Boethius wrote theological works in which he pioneered a method of explaining theological claims using the tools of philosophy. All of these theological writings are entirely orthodox. They suggest, at the very least, that Boethius's overall attitude to philosophy was not antagonistic.

One of the things nearly all Christian theologians agree on is that some of the articles of their religion cannot be *proved* by the methods of philosophy or science or history or any other discipline. But proof is a high bar. To deny that philosophy can prove

7. Relihan, *Prisoner's Philosophy*, 84–92.
8. Relihan, *Prisoner's Philosophy*, 91–93.

that God is a Trinity or that Jesus Christ is fully God and fully man is a long way from denying that philosophy has a constructive place in Christian life and theological inquiry.

At the end of the last chapter, I asked some of the questions that Lady Philosophy, for all her wisdom, cannot answer. But I judge her work a success. She helped a man who had long training in philosophy to remember some of the valuable lessons the philosophers have to offer, including the centrality of virtue to the happy life and the importance of not identifying our happiness with the goods of fortune. Having helped him out of his depressive state, she puzzles with him over hard questions that arise given his faith commitments: Is God really good? Can happiness be found in God? Why is there evil if God is good? Will God permit injustice to go unpunished forever? Is there room for freedom in the working out of God's grand plan for the world?

Few religious people have asked these questions sincerely and failed to get at least a little worked up about them. Theology, of course, has a lot to say in answer to these questions. But so does philosophy. And in certain states of mind, questions about religion that threaten religious commitment itself cannot be beneficially answered by the theological resources of religion. Boethius the author tested the limits of philosophy's potential for addressing these questions. His character Lady Philosophy, spurred on by her dialogue partner, made it very far indeed. Just not far enough.

Those readers who follow Lady Philosophy to her limits are faced with a choice: either the questions she can't answer simply can't be answered, or they can be answered but by a subject, or a someone, beyond philosophy. If Lady Philosophy represents all of human wisdom, this thing beyond philosophy transcends what we humans can know or believe by our own efforts.

THE UNINTERESTING QUESTION

I have criticized Relihan's satirical reading of *Consolation*, but I do appreciate one of its clever ironies: it opposes a long and obstinate tradition of reading the *Consolation* as evidence that Boethius, deep down, was at best nominally Christian. In his moment of crisis, he turned to philosophy rather than religion, and this reveals his true allegiance.

In the middle of the twentieth century, the iconoclastic Jesuit Herbert Thurston undertook a revision of Alban Butler's beloved *Lives of the Saints*. Part of the justification for a new edition was that the Church had produced many saints since the eighteenth century. But Thurston took the opportunity to add to or alter Butler's original entries. To the entry on Boethius, Thurston added a long section casting some doubt on Boethius's martyrdom and even his faith. "How is it," he asks, "that a Christian man, who had written treatises in defence of the faith, should, in face of an unjust charge and of death, write a work for his own strengthening and solace which contains nothing distinctively Christian except one or two indirect quotations from the Bible?"[9]

The question is unserious and uninteresting. We don't know what else he was doing in prison besides composing the *Consolation*. Maybe he smoked some cigarettes or played chess. Maybe he scratched lines on the walls, one for each day. Maybe he read the Bible and the writings of saints and Church Fathers for his edification. Maybe he spent hours a day in fervent prayer. Maybe he had planned a companion volume, the *Consolation of Theology*, but ran out of time. We just have no idea. (Okay, we know he wasn't smoking or playing chess, because those weren't around in sixth-century Italy.) Even if the *Consolation* had *nothing* to do with theology, it is still an acceptable thing for a Christian man to put his secular expertise to work. Must the imprisoned Christian artist sketch only sacred images? Why not a bird in a tree or the shadows

9. Butler, *Lives of the Saints*, ed. Thurston and Attwater, 4:183.

cast by bars of iron? But *Consolation* in fact has a *great deal* to do with theology, as you now know if you have made it this far.

Here is a permissible and even pious attitude for a Christian sometimes to adopt: I have staked my life on my faith. It shapes everything I do. I hope it's true. Lots of people think it's false and offer some reasonable objections. Can those objections be overcome? The responsible thing to do is to try to answer the questions as well as you can, without fear or dishonesty. You will not find certainty this way. But you might find some consolation.

That is more or less how I imagine Boethius's efforts in the *Consolation* fitting into his religious life. In this way, I stake a middle ground between Relihan and Thurston. Whereas Relihan thinks *Consolation* is a Christian book insofar as it is anti-philosophical, Thurston thinks it is an anti-Christian book insofar as it is philosophical. They can't both be right, but they can both be partially right: it is a Christian book insofar as it is philosophical—while reasonably acknowledging the limits of philosophy.

THE GOSPEL ACCORDING TO BOETHIUS

Boethius wrote five short theological treatises, which were sometimes published together with *Consolation* in the early centuries after his death.[10] For our purposes, the fourth treatise is of most interest. It is an unapologetic statement of the Christian faith. It reads almost like a long creed; its structure follows the Apostle's Creed. No one reading it, knowing nothing else of its author, would have any reason to doubt that its author meant what he said.

The Christian faith, he professes, is proclaimed by the authority of the Bible, the New Testament and the Old.[11] The advent of Christ is prophesied in the Old and revealed in the New.

10. Troncarelli, "Afterword," in *Companion to Boethius*, ed. Kaylor and Phillips, 539.
11. Boethius, Tractate 4: *De fide catholica*, in *Theological Tractates*, trans. Stewart et al., 53.

The foundational doctrine of this religion is its doctrine of God: "From eternity, that is, before the establishment of the world, before all, that is, that can be given the name of time, there has existed the divine substance of Father, Son, and Holy Spirit in such wise that our religion calls the Father God, the Son God, and the Holy Spirit God, and yet not three Gods but one."[12]

This triune God, eternal and unified in mind and will, decided to make the world. The world is not fashioned out of pre-existing materials, nor is it fashioned out of the divine substance itself, as though it were itself divine. He did not fashion the world by looking to any model—unlike the god or "demiurge" of Plato's *Timaeus*, who looks to the Forms as the model for the world he shapes[13]—but by his own word (*verbum*).

The world God created was and is good. But men rebelled, tempted by the leader of the fallen angels. The first man and first woman were punished for their disobedience by expulsion from the earthly paradise.

The human race inherited the punishment of its first parents and fell deeper into wickedness and misery. To save this sinful world, God ordained the Blessed Virgin Mary to bear in her womb "the Maker of the human race."[14] Her child is "the Son of Man and likewise the Son of God that in him the glory of the divine nature might shine forth and at the same time his assumption of human weakness be made clear."[15]

This man, Jesus Christ, ministered on earth, gathering the twelve Apostles, instructing them about his saving mission. Religious authorities rejected his ministry and killed him by crucifixion. But three days later, he rose from the dead, "as he had predetermined with his Father before the foundation of the world"—the ultimate eucatastrophe. He ascended into heaven, a

12. Boethius, *De fide catholica*, in *Theological Tractates*, trans. Stewart et al., 53.
13. Plato, *Timaeus* 28a–b.
14. Boethius, *De fide catholica*, in *Theological Tractates*, trans. Stewart et al., 65.
15. Boethius, *De fide catholica*, in *Theological Tractates*, trans. Stewart et al., 65.

heaven he never truly left, giving a sign for all the world that our ultimate destiny lies somewhere beyond the confines of this world. He deputized his twelve Apostles to continue his ministry of evangelization and healing, instituting "certain health-giving sacraments" that mankind might receive and know divine grace.[16]

Christ's Apostles took up their mission, spreading Christ's teaching throughout the world, forming all men into "one Body," the Church. This teaching, which "instructs this present life in good works," promises that "after the end of the world our bodies shall rise incorruptible to the kingdom of heaven," where we shall be judged, those who have lived rightly by grace rewarded with beatitude, and the wicked punished with misery. The blessed will reside in "that heavenly city of which the Virgin's Son is King and where will be everlasting joy, delight, food, labour, and unending praise of the Creator."[17]

This glorious hope cannot be discerned solely through natural investigative methods. It requires *faith*—a faith Boethius describes as the mind's assenting meditation on the good that is revealed to it concerning what is hidden about the past, present, and future.[18]

Philosophy, grasped through reason, can get us to the hope that there is a God who is wise and good and who therefore will make all good. But theology, grasped by faith, fills out and extends that hope: in Jesus, the man of sorrows, above all, we see the "firstfruits" of God's awesome plan—eternal life of joyful communion with God.[19]

It is good to dwell on the sort of answer faith gives us: a divine person suffers with us and promises that it will all be worth it in the end.[20] You cannot syllogize your way to God's ultimate

---

16. Boethius, *De fide catholica*, in *Theological Tractates*, trans. Stewart et al., 69.
17. Boethius, *De fide catholica*, in *Theological Tractates*, trans. Stewart et al., 71.
18. Troncarelli, "Mentis Cogitatio," in *Les prologues médiévaux*, ed. Hamesse, 43.
19. 1 Corinthians 15:23 (King James Version).
20. See John 10:10.

reasons for permitting you to suffer. For that matter, you cannot syllogize your way to God's ultimate reasons for permitting you to be happy. In the deepest possible way, you don't *deserve* either suffering or happiness, because you don't *deserve* existence itself. Yet here you are. You might not have been. The Author of the story of the world wanted you to be on the scene, and to be saved when the curtain falls.[21] To questions about how or why God would allow this or that to happen to you, given his grand plan, his reply is Jesus, who "for the joy that was set before him endured the cross, despising the shame, and is seated at the right hand of the throne of God."[22]

ST. SEVERINUS

There is a church in Pavia, Italy, that Boethius might have seen under construction. The church is dedicated to the first pope, St. Peter, and it is called San Pietro in Ciel d'Oro (St. Peter in Golden Heaven). Maybe Boethius entertained the thought that his mortal remains might one day be interred there or in its vicinity; probably he did not entertain the thought that he would one day be honored there as a martyr. But so he is. You can go there and see for yourself. I hope to do so someday.

There is a long poem written in Ravenna, Italy, eight hundred years after Boethius's death. The poem tells the story of a man's journey through the spheres of Paradise. Along the way, he stops in the sphere of saintly philosophers and theologians. He strikes up a conversation with St. Thomas Aquinas, who introduces him to the brightest luminaries in the sphere. Over there, says St. Thomas, "Because / He saw that all was good, now in delight / shimmers that spirit who made manifest / how the world cheats— to all who hear him right. / The flesh whence he was driven lies at

21. See 1 Timothy 2:4.
22. Hebrews 12:2.

rest / in the crypts of Ciel d'Oro; but he came / from martyrdom and exile to this peace."[23] This holy soul, of course, is Boethius. And the poet who put him in this lofty heaven is Dante.

Boethius wrote *Consolation* in prison, uncertain of when he would die but confident he would die soon. Of the gruesome manner of his martyrdom, Edward Gibbon wrote, "Suspense, the worst of evils, was at length determined by the ministers of death, who executed, and perhaps exceeded, the inhuman mandate of Theoderic. A strong cord was fastened round the head of Boethius, and forcibly tightened till his eyes almost started from their sockets; and some mercy may be discovered in the milder torture of beating him with clubs till he expired."[24]

The people of Pavia didn't need to be told that they had a saint and a martyr on their hands. He has been revered in the town of his death pretty much since the day he died. Today, in the crypt below the sanctuary of San Pietro in Ciel d'Oro, the inscription "The body of St. Severinus Boethius, martyr" adorns a white marble sarcophagus. In front of the sarcophagus is a small altar. A plaque nearby offers a short biography of this man "great and altogether worthy to be praised."[25] Alban Butler acknowledged this long custom in his original *Lives of the Saints* and in 1883 Rome formally recognized the sanctity of St. Severinus Boethius.[26] He is commemorated in the most recent edition of the *Martyrologium Romanum*, the Church's official record of those who have died for the faith.[27] The day of his memorial is October 23.

23. Dante, *Paradise* 10.124–29, trans. Esolen, 107.

24. Gibbon, *Decline and Fall*, 7:52.

25. DiPippo, "The Relics of St Boethius."

26. *Acta Sanctae Sedis* 16:302–3.

27. *Martyrologium Romanum*, 586.

Acknowledgments

I am grateful to my students over the years who have pushed me to go deeper into Boethius than I might otherwise have done; to my friend Matthew Lee Anderson for Boethian intrigue over pints at Pinewood; to Dylan, Austin, Emma, and the rest of the staff at Pinewood, for pouring those pints and fostering a third place of genuine care; to David Augustine, my editor at Word on Fire Academic, for his encouragement, patience, and tolerance of risk; to my wife, Katie, and our children, for letting me use my sabbatical rather less restfully than originally planned; and finally, to Boethius himself, for his books and for the testimony of his life. St. Severinus Boethius, pray for us.

Bibliography

Acta Sanctae Sedis. Vol. 16. Edited by Iosephi Pennacchi and Victorii Piazzesi. Rome: Typographia Polyglotta, 1906.

Aertsen, Jan A. *Medieval Philosophy as Transcendental Thought: From Philip the Chancellor (ca. 1225) to Francisco Suárez.* Leiden, NL: Brill, 2012.

Alighieri, Dante. *Inferno.* Translated and edited by Anthony Esolen. New York: Modern Library, 2003.

———. *Paradise.* Translated and edited by Anthony Esolen. New York: Modern Library, 2007.

Annas, Julia. *The Morality of Happiness.* Reprint ed. Oxford: Oxford University Press, 1995.

Anselm of Canterbury. *Basic Writings.* Edited and translated by Thomas Williams. Indianapolis, IN: Hackett, 2007.

Aristophanes. *Four Plays: "The Clouds," "The Birds," "Lysistrata," "The Frogs."* Translated by William Arrowsmith, Richmond Lattimore, and Douglass Parker. New York: Meridian, 1994.

Aristotle. *The Complete Works of Aristotle.* 2 vols. Edited by Jonathan Barnes. Princeton, NJ: Princeton University Press, 1984.

Asbell, William J., Jr. "The Philosophical Background of *Sufficientia* in Boethius's *Consolation,* Book 3." In *New Directions in Boethian Studies,* edited by Noel Harold Kaylor Jr. and Philip Edward Phillips, 3–16. Kalamazoo, MI: Medieval Institute, 2007.

Augustine of Hippo. *The City of God against the Pagans.* Translated and edited by R.W. Dyson. Cambridge: Cambridge University Press, 1998.

———. *Confessions.* Translated by Henry Chadwick. Oxford: Oxford University Press, 1992.

Augustine of Hippo. *On Free Choice of the Will*. Translated by Thomas Williams. Indianapolis, IN: Hackett, 1993.

———. *De moribus Ecclesiae catholicae et de moribus Manichaeorum, Libri Duo*. Patrologia Latina 32, edited by J.P. Migne. Paris, 1845.

Baggett, David, and Jerry L. Walls. *Good God: The Theistic Foundations of Morality*. Oxford: Oxford University Press, 2011.

Bellarmine, Robert. *The Ascent of the Mind to God: By the Ladder of Creation*. Translated by Ryan Grant. Post Falls, ID: Mediatrix Press, 2022.

Benatar, David. *Better Never to Have Been: The Harm of Coming Into Existence*. Oxford: Clarendon Press, 2006.

Bernard of Clairvaux. "On Loving God." In *Selected Works*, translated by G.R. Evans, 173–206. New York: Paulist, 1987.

Blake, William. *Poems*. New York: Alfred A. Knopf, 1994.

Bobzien, Susanne. "Frege Plagiarized the Stoics." In *Themes in Plato, Aristotle, and Hellenistic Philosophy: Keeling Lectures 2011–18*, edited by Fiona Leigh, 149–206. London: University of London Press, 2021.

Boethius. *The Consolation of Philosophy*. Translated by Scott Goins and Barbara H. Wyman. San Francisco: Ignatius, 2012.

———. *Consolation of Philosophy*. Translated by Joel C. Relihan. Indianapolis, IN: Hackett, 2001.

———. *The Consolation of Philosophy*. Rev. ed. Translated by Victor Watts. New York: Penguin, 1999.

———. *The Theological Tractates. The Consolation of Philosophy*. Translated by H.F. Stewart, E.K. Rand, and S.J. Tester. Loeb Classical Library 74. Cambridge, MA: Harvard University Press, 1973.

Bolt, Robert. *A Man for All Seasons: A Play in Two Acts*. New York: Vintage International, 1990.

Bonaventure. *Itinerarium mentis in Deum*. Edited by Philotheus Boehner and Zachary Hayes. Translated by Zachary Hayes. Vol. 2 of *Works of St. Bonaventure*. NY: Franciscan Institute, 2002.

The Book of Common Prayer. Amended 1662 ed. Cambridge: Cambridge University Press, 2003.

Buras, Todd, and Michael Cantrell. "C.S. Lewis's Argument from Nostalgia: A New Argument from Desire." In *Two Dozen (or so) Arguments for God: The Plantinga Project*, edited by Jerry L. Walls and Trent Dougherty, 356–71. Oxford: Oxford University Press, 2018.

Butler, Alban. *Lives of the Saints*. 4 vols. Edited by Herbert J. Thurston and Donald Attwater. Westminster, MD: Christian Classics, 1981.

Camus, Albert. *The Stranger*. Translated by Stuart Gilbert. New York: Alfred A. Knopf, 1967.

Carr, Nicholas. *The Shallows: What the Internet Is Doing to Our Brains*. New York: W.W. Norton, 2011.

Carson, Rachel. *Silent Spring*. New York: Fawcett Crest, 1962.

Chadwick, Henry. *Boethius: The Consolations of Music, Logic, Theology, and Philosophy*. Oxford: Oxford University Press, 1981.

Chesterton, G.K. *The Collected Works of G.K. Chesterton*. Vol. 10, *Collected Poetry, Part III*. Edited by Denis J. Conlon. San Francisco: Ignatius, 2010.

Cicero. *De finibus bonorum et malorum*. Translated by H. Rackham. Loeb Classical Library 40. Cambridge, MA: Harvard University Press, 1914.

Coleridge, Samuel Taylor. *Biographia Literaria*, edited by James Engell and W. Jackson Bate. Vol. 7, part 1 of *The Collected Works of Samuel Taylor Coleridge*. Princeton, NJ: Princeton University Press, 1983.

Crouch, Andy. *The Life We're Looking For: Reclaiming Relationship in a Technological World*. New York: Convergent Books, 2022.

De Beauvoir, Simone. *The Second Sex*. Translated by Constance Borde and Sheila Malovany-Chevallier. New York: Vintage Books, 2009.

Descartes, René. *Meditations on First Philosophy: With Selections from the Objections and Replies*. Edited and translated by John Cottingham. Cambridge: Cambridge University Press, 1996

Dickens, Charles. *A Christmas Carol and Other Christmas Writings*. London: Penguin Classics, 2003.

Diogenes Laertius. *The Lives and Opinions of Eminent Philosophers*. Translated by C.D. Yonge. London: G. Bell & Sons, 1915.

DiPippo, Gregory. "The Relics of St Boethius." *New Liturgical Movement,* October 23, 2019. https://www.newliturgicalmovement.org/2019/10/the-relics-of-st-boethius.html.

Drogula, Fred K. *Cato the Younger: Life and Death at the End of the Roman Republic*. Oxford: Oxford University Press, 2019.

Duns Scotus, John. *Treatise on the First Principle*. Translated by Thomas M. Ward. Indianapolis, IN: Hackett, 2024.

Ehrlich, Paul R. *The Population Bomb*. San Francisco: Sierra Club, 1969.

Eliot, T.S. *Four Quartets*. New York: Harcourt, Brace, 1943.

Emerson, Ralph Waldo. *Poems*. Vol. 9 of *The Works of Ralph Waldo Emerson*, Fireside edition. Boston: 1909.

Epictetus. *The Complete Works: Handbook, Discourses, and Fragments*. Edited and translated by Robin Waterfield. Chicago: University of Chicago Press, 2022.

Ford, John C. *Man Takes a Drink: Facts and Principles About Alcohol*. New York: P.J. Kenedy & Sons, 1955.

Foucault, Michel. *The History of Sexuality*. Vol. 1, *An Introduction*, translated by Robert Hurley. New York: Pantheon Books, 1978.

Frankl, Viktor E. *Yes to Life: In Spite of Everything*. Boston: Beacon, 2019.

Freud, Sigmund. *Civilization and its Discontents*. Translated by James Strachey. New York: W.W. Norton, 2010.

Gibbon, Edward. *The History of the Decline and Fall of the Roman Empire*. 8 vols. London: T. Cadell, 1838.

Greenblatt, Stephen. *The Swerve: How the World Became Modern*. New York: W.W. Norton, 2011.

Gruber, Joachim. *Kommentar zu Boethius, "De consolatione philosophiae."* Berlin: De Gruyter, 2006.

Harari, Yuval Noah. *Homo Deus: A Brief History of Tomorrow*. London: Harvill Secker, 2016.

Herodotus. *The Landmark Herodotus: The Histories*. Edited by Robert B. Strassler. Translated by Andrea L. Purvis. New York: Vintage Books, 2009.

Herold, Christine. "Boethius's *Consolatione Philosophiae* as a Bridge Between Classical and Christian Conceptions of Tragedy." In *New Directions in Boethian Studies*, edited by Noel Harold Kaylor Jr. and Philip Edward Phillips, 17–32. Kalamazoo, MI: Medieval Institute, 2007.

Hildebrand, Tyler, and Thomas Metcalf. "The Nomological Argument for the Existence of God." *Noûs* 56, no. 2 (2021): 443–72.

Hitz, Zena. *Lost in Thought: The Hidden Pleasures of an Intellectual Life*. Princeton, NJ: Princeton University Press, 2020.

Holmes, Michael W., ed. *The Apostolic Fathers*. 2nd ed. Translated by J.B. Lightfoot and J.R. Harmer. Grand Rapids, MI: Baker Book House, 1989.

Homer. *The Odyssey*. Translated by Robert Fagles. New York, Penguin, 1999.

John of the Cross. *Selected Poems*. Translated by Terence O'Reilly. Cambridge: Iona, 2021.

Kim, Kyeezu, Brian T. Joyce, Drew R. Nannini, Yinan Zheng, Penny Gordon-Larsen, James M. Shikany, Donald M. Lloyd-Jones, Ming Hu, Mark J. Nieuwenhuijsen, Douglas E. Vaughan, Kai Zhang, and Lifang Hou. "Inequalities in Urban Greenness and Epigenetic Aging: Different Associations by Race and Neighborhood Socio-Economic Status." *Science Advances* 9, no. 26 (2023).

Klee, Miles. "Millionaire Biohacker Says Algorithm Runs His Life: 'My Mind No Longer Decides'" *Rolling Stone*, September 11, 2023. https://www.rollingstone.com/culture/culture-features/bryan-johnson-anti-aging-blueprint-algorithm-1234821163/.

Lewis, C.S. *The Discarded Image: An Introduction to Medieval and Renaissance Literature*. Cambridge: Cambridge University Press, 1964.

———. *The Great Divorce: A Dream*. New York: HarperOne, 1946.

———. *The Last Battle*. In Lewis, *The Chronicles of Narnia*, 665–767. New York: HarperCollins, 1982.

———. *Perelandra*. In Lewis, *The Space Trilogy*. New York: Scribner, 2011.

———. *The Pilgrim's Regress*. Grand Rapids, MI: Eerdmans, 1958.

———. *Poems*. New York: HarperCollins, 2017.

———. *Prince Caspian*. In Lewis, *The Chronicles of Narnia*, 311–418. New York: HarperCollins, 1982.

———. *The Problem of Pain*. New York: HarperCollins, 2001.

———. *Till We Have Faces: A Myth Retold*. San Francisco: HarperOne, 2017.

———. *Voyage of the Dawn Treader*. In Lewis, *The Chronicles of Narnia*, 419–542. New York: HarperCollins, 1982.

Long, A.A. *From Epicurus to Epictetus: Studies in Hellenistic and Roman Philosophy.* Oxford: Clarendon, 2006.

Long, A.A., and D.N. Sedley. *The Hellenistic Philosophers.* Vol. 1, *Translations of the Principal Sources, with Philosophical Commentary.* Cambridge: Cambridge University Press, 1987.

Lucretius. *On the Nature of Things.* Translated by Charles E. Bennett. Roslyn, NY: Walter J. Black, 1946.

MacDonald, George. *Lilith.* Whitethorn, CA: Johannesen, 1994.

———. *The Princess and Curdie.* London: J.M. Dent & Sons, 1949.

———. *Phantastes.* Grand Rapids, MI: Eerdmans, 2000.

Mackie, J.L. *Ethics: Inventing Right and Wrong.* Harmondsworth, UK: Penguin Books, 1977.

Malla, Ashok, Ridha Joober, and Amparo Garcia. "'Mental Illness Is Like Any Other Medical Illness': A Critical Examination of the Statement and Its Impact on Patient Care and Society." *Journal of Psychiatry and Neuroscience* 40, no. 3 (2015): 147–50.

Marcus Aurelius. *Meditations.* Translated by A.S.L. Farquharson. Oxford: Oxford University Press, 1989. Marenbon, John. *Boethius.* Oxford: Oxford University Press, 2003.

———. *Pagans and Philosophers: The Problem of Paganism from Augustine to Leibniz.* Princeton, NJ: Princeton University Press, 2015.

Martyrologium Romanum. Vatican City: Typis Vaticanis, 2004.

Marx, Karl, and Friedrich Engels. *The Communist Manifesto.* In Karl Marx, *Selected Writings*, 2nd ed., edited by David McLellan, 245–72. Oxford: Oxford University Press, 2005.

McCracken, Brett. "Should You Quit Netflix?" *The Gospel Coalition*, June 19, 2019. https://www.thegospelcoalition.org/article/quit-netflix/.

McDougall G.J. "What Role Philosophy in Psychotherapy?" *Perspectives in Psychiatric Care* 28, no. 2 (1992): 3.

McKirahan, Richard D., Jr. *Philosophy Before Socrates: An Introduction with Texts and Commentary*. Indianapolis, IN: Hackett, 1994.

Merton, Thomas. *Contemplative Prayer*. New York: Herder & Herder, 1969.

Nozick, Robert. *Anarchy, State, and Utopia*. New York: Basic Books, 1974.

Nietzsche, Friedrich. *On the "Genealogy of Morals" and "Ecce Homo."* Translated by Walter Kaufmann and R.J. Hollingdale. Edited by Walter Kaufmann. New York: Vintage Books, 1989.

Paley, William. *Natural Theology, or Evidence of the Existence and Attributes of the Deity, collected from the appearances of nature*. Edited by Matthew D. Eddy and David Knight. Oxford: Oxford University Press, 2006.

Pelikan, Jaroslav. *The Emergence of the Catholic Tradition (100–600)*. Vol. 1 of *The Christian Tradition: A History of the Development of the Catholic Tradition (100–600)*. Chicago: University of Chicago Press, 1971.

Phillips, Philip Edward. "The English Tradition of Boethius's *De consolatione philosophiae* with a Checklist of Translations." In *Vernacular Traditions of Boethius's "De consolatione philosophiae,"* edited by Noel Harold Kaylor Jr. and Philip Edward Phillips, 221–49. Kalamazoo, MI: Medieval Institute, 2015.

Plantinga, Alvin. *God, Freedom, and Evil*. Grand Rapids, MI: Eerdmans, 1977.

Plato. *Complete Works*. Edited by John M. Cooper. Indianapolis, IN: Hackett, 1997.

Plutarch. *Lives*. Vol. 7, translated by Bernadotte Perrin. Loeb Classical Library 99. Cambridge, MA: Harvard University Press, 1919.

Plutarch. *Moralia*. Vol. 6, translated by W.C. Helmbold. Loeb Classical Library 337. Cambridge, MA: Harvard University Press, 1939.

Postman, Neil. *Amusing Ourselves to Death: Public Discourse in the Age of Show Business*. New York: Penguin, 1985.

Poston, Ted. "The Argument from (A) to (Y): The Argument from So Many Arguments." In *Two Dozen (or So) Arguments for God: The Plantinga Project*, edited by Jerry L. Walls and Trent Dougherty, 372–88. Oxford: Oxford University Press, 2018.

Reiss, Edmund. *Boethius*. Boston: Twayne, 1982.

Relihan, Joel C. *The Prisoner's Philosophy: Life and Death in Boethius's "Consolation."* Notre Dame, IN: University of Notre Dame Press, 2007.

Rosenberg, Alex. *The Atheist's Guide to Reality: Enjoying Life without Illusions*. New York: W.W. Norton, 2011.

Rota, Michael. "Why Is the Universe Just Right for Life?" in *Taking Pascal's Wager: Faith, Evidence, and the Abundant Life*, 99–112. Downers Grove, IL: IVP Academic, 2016.

Rowling, J.K. *Harry Potter and the Deathly Hallows*. New York: Arthur A. Levine Books, 2007.

Sandbach, F.H. *The Stoics*. 2nd ed. Indianapolis, IN: Hackett, 1994.

Saunders, Jason L., ed. *Greek and Roman Philosophy after Aristotle*. New York: Free Press, 1966.

Saxbe, Darby. "This Is Not the Way to Help Depressed Teenagers." *The New York Times*, November 18, 2023. https://www.nytimes.com/2023/11/18/opinion/teenagers-mental-health-treatment.html.

Sayers, Dorothy L. *Gaudy Night*. New York: HarperTorch, 2006.

Schopenhauer, Arthur. *The World as Will and Representation*. 2 vols. Translated by E.F.J. Payne. New York: Dover, 1969.

Schwartz, Jeffrey M., and Rebecca Gladding. *You Are Not Your Brain: The 4-Step Solution for Changing Bad Habits, Ending Unhealthy Thinking, and Taking Control of Your Life*. New York: Penguin, 2011.

Sedgefield, Walter John. *King Alfred's Version of the Consolations of Boethius, Done into Modern English*. Oxford: Clarendon, 1900.

Seneca. *Moral Letters to Lucilius*. Translated by Richard M. Gummere. Ottawa: Stoici Civitas Press, 2013.

————. *On Tranquility of Mind*. In Seneca, *On the Shortness of Life*, translated by C.D.N. Costa, 68–106. New York: Penguin, 1997.

Sextus Empiricus. *Selections from the Major Writings on Scepticism, Man, & God*. Edited by Philip P. Hallie. Translated by Sanford G. Etheridge. Indianapolis, IN: Hackett, 1985.

Shakespeare, William. *Hamlet*. London: Penguin, 1996.

Shanzer, Danuta. "Interpreting the *Consolation*." In *The Cambridge Companion to Boethius*, ed. John Marenbon, 228–54. Cambridge: Cambridge University Press, 2009.

Solzhenitsyn, Aleksandr I. *The Gulag Archipelago 1918–1956: An Experiment in Literary Investigation, III–IV*. Translated by Thomas P. Whitney. New York: Harper & Row, 1973.

Stanton, Glenn. "FactChecker: C.S. Lewis and G.K. Chesterton Quotes." *The Gospel Coalition*, April 14, 2013. https://www.thegospelcoalition.org/article/factchecker-c-s-lewis-and-g-k-chesterton-quotes/.

Strawson, Galen. "The Consciousness Deniers." *The New York Review*, March 13, 2018. https://www.nybooks.com/online/2018/03/13/the-consciousness-deniers/.

Swinburne, Richard. *The Existence of God*. 2nd ed. Oxford: Clarendon Press, 2004.

Taylor, Charles. *A Secular Age*. Cambridge, MA: Belknap, 2007.

Thomas Aquinas. *Aquinas: Basic Works*. Edited by Jeffrey Hause and Robert Pasnau. Indianapolis, IN: Hackett, 2014.

———. *De regno ad regem Cypri*. Translated by Gerald B. Phelan and revised by I.T. Eschmann. Toronto: Pontifical Institute of Mediaeval Studies, 1949.

Tolkien, J.R.R. *The Lord of the Rings*. Boston: Houghton Mifflin, 2004.

———. "On Fairy-stories." In Tolkien, *Tales from the Perilous Realm*, 313–400. Boston: Houghton Mifflin Harcourt, 2008.

———. *The Silmarillion*. New York: Ballantine Books, 1979.

Troncarelli, Fabio. "Afterword: Boethius in Late Antiquity and the Early Middle Ages." In *A Companion to Boethius in the Middle Ages*, edited by Noel Harold Kaylor Jr. and Philip Edward Phillips, 519–49. Leiden, NL: Brill, 2012.

———. "Mentis Cogitatio: Un Prologo di Boezio in un Prologo a Boezio?" In *Les prologues médiévaux*, edited by Jacqueline Hamesse, 39–86. Textes et Études du Moyen Âge 15. Turnhout, BE: Brepols, 2000.

———. "New Words on Boethius." *Carmina Philosophiae* 23 (2014): 1–11.

Waldinger, Robert, and Marc Schulz. *The Good Life: Lessons from the World's Longest Scientific Study of Happiness*. New York: Simon & Schuster, 2023.

Whitehead, A.N. *Process and Reality: An Essay in Cosmology*. Corrected ed. Edited by David Ray Griffin and Donald W. Sherburne. New York: Free Press, 1978.

Williams, Bernard. "The Makropulos Case: Reflections on the Tedium of Immortality." In Williams, *Problems of the Self*, 82–100. Cambridge: Cambridge University Press, 1973.

Index